30 DAYS WITH
JESUS

Donielle Ingersoll

Printed in the United States of America

LCCN:		2021904091
ISBN:	Softcover	978-1-64908-900-7
	eBook	978-1-64908-899-4

Republished by: PageTurner Press and Media LLC
Publication Date: 03/10/2021

To order copies of this book, contact:

PageTurner Press and Media
Phone: 1-888-447-9651
order@pageturner.us
www.pageturner.us

PREFACE

While having morning devotions, I ran across a statement from a sermon, a dedicated servant of God gave in Sweden on June 27, 1886. During the message, Enoch was mentioned. I have always been interested in Enoch and the walk he had with God. The Bible states Enoch was translated to heaven without seeing death. He is the oldest, continually living, human being in the history of mankind. His age is somewhere between five and six thousand years. Most of that time he has spent in heaven or other parts of the vast universe of God.

Is it possible for men and women today to walk with God as Enoch did? According to this section of the sermon, yes, it is. In writing this book it is my desire that you, Reader, understand: (1) What it means to walk and talk with God. (2) What you are to do while walking and talking with God. (3) What you can expect to happen while you are walking and talking with God. Below is the statement that spoke volumes to my quest to walk the Enoch walk with God.

While we are in this world, we are not safe unless our petitions are continually

1

ascend ing to the God of heaven that He will keep us unspotted from the corruption of the world. Our Saviour has told us what would be in these last days. Iniquity will abound, but the souls that are open to the influence of the Spirit of God will receive strength to withstand the corruptions of this degenerate age.

Enoch walked with God three hundred years before his translation to heaven, and the state of the world was not then more favorable for the perfection of Christian character than it is today. And how did Enoch walk with God? He educated his mind and heart to ever feel that he was in the presence of God, and when in perplexity his prayers would ascend to God to keep him, he refused to take any course that would offend his God. He kept the Lord continually before Him. He would pray, "Teach me Thy way, that I may not err. What is Thy pleasure concerning me? What shall I do to honor Thee, my God?" Thus, he was constantly shaping his way and course in accordance with God's commandments, and he had perfect confidence and trust in his heavenly Father, that He would help him. He had no thought or will of his own; it was all submerged in the will of his Father.

Now, Enoch was a representative of those who will be upon the earth when Christ shall come, who will be translated to heaven without seeing death. But be sure that if your hearts are inclined not to do God's will, not to keep the way of the Lord but to follow your own way, then you are not in harmony with the God of heaven. Volume 1, Sermons and Talks p. 32

30 DAYS WITH JESUS

Day One

For several days now, I have felt an urgent need to draw closer to Jesus. I do not want a surface friendship, but a remarkably close and personal one. I have read of men and women who drew so close to Jesus that they walked and talked with Him and He with them. This was the type of friendship I am searching for. I want Jesus to walk with me. I have been working on this off and on for several years. In the past, I usually started out fine, but after a couple of hours forgot that Jesus was walking with me. It has been that way for much of my life. Today was different though. Today we walked together. When I went up town, He road along with me. I even opened the patssenger door for Him and made sure the seat was clear of things so He could be comfortable. We had a great day together.

One subject that we discussed was the reality of His presence. Just how present is Jesus with us? He is very present. He brought a Bible text to my mind. It is found in the last part of Matthew 28:20, *"Lo, I am with you always, even unto the end of the world."* Last time I checked, the world had not ended yet so that means Jesus really is with me and He is with you, too. He is

1

so present with us there is no where we can go to get away from Him. David puts it this way in Psalm 139:7-10, *"Whither shall I go from thy spirit? or whither shall I flee from thy presence? If I ascend into heaven, thou art there: if I make my bed in hell, behold, thou art there. If I take the wings of the morning, and dwell in the uttermost parts of the sea; Even there shall thy hand lead me, and thy right hand shall hold me."* (KJV) We talked about a lot of things. There were a few times either going to or returning from town when He pointed out some people to me. I talked to Him about them. The normal term for that would have been pray for them, but since Jesus was traveling with me, we talked about them. We talked about some of my acquaintances also. It was so rewarding to entrust them to His care and keeping.

Perhaps you would appreciate knowing how to make your friendship with Jesus more fulfilling. If so, come on in and sit down. The three of us can discuss it together. Now for introductions, Jesus knows you much better than I do. He loves you very, very much. In fact, do you know that Jesus loves you more than He loves Himself? Really! It is true! His own words testify to this fact. *"Greater love hath no man than this, that a man lay down his life for a friend."* John 15:13. (KJV) Jesus loves you more than He loves Himself and He proved it when He laid down His life for you on the cross. You might ask, why? Because He is your Maker. He planned just how He would create you long ago. Even before you were born, He knew all about you. Continuing in Psalm 139.14-18 (NLT) *"Thank you for making me so wonderfully complex! Your workmanship is marvelous-and how well I know it. You watched me as I was being formed in utter seclusion, as I was woven together in the dark of the womb. You saw me before I was born. Every day of my life was recorded in your book. Every moment was laid out before a single day had passed. How precious are your thoughts about me, O God! they are innumerable! I cannot even count them; they outnumber the grains of sand! And when I wake up in the morning, you are still with me!"* This is only the beginning, too. Jesus not only made you, but He also wants you to be His bride, forever. So, you see, Jesus knows you very well, loves you more than you can possibly understand, and really is with you always, even while you are sleeping. Since He knows you so well, we are not strangers, but brothers and sisters through Him.

I will briefly introduce myself to you now. My name is Donielle Ingersoll. I have been a Christian all my life. I attended Christian schools and had loving parents who prayed for me daily. In 1978 I graduated from Andrews University with a master's degree in Art. At that time, I received certification to teach on the Secondary level. While going to college, I started a landscape business and have continued in that occupation for over 30 years. I have a wife and one son. We live in Washington. We are active church members. The Lord has blessed us. He has given me a great deal of creativity. I have used it in hundreds of ways. Writing is one of those ways. This is the third complete book I have written. My first book is called "*A Little Taste of Heaven*" My second was a study in Daniel and Revelation. There are other books that I have published along with some about half written. I never planned to write but once while talking to Jesus, He told me to write. I argued with Him about it for a while and told Him if He wanted me to write that I needed a computer. This was several years ago before they were so popular. I was landscaping at the time and received a call for an estimate that very afternoon. The individual worked at Heath Company in St. Joseph, Michigan. He paid for a portion of the landscaping with a Zenith computer. I took it home before I ever started the job. I had no excuse after that.

Writing is more creative than reading. Rather than settle for how the author thinks things should begin and end, as a writer I can determine these things. Well not entirely. Since Jesus is with us always, His input is most important. This journey we are on, hopefully for many days to come can end in several ways. I do not have an ending planned. Neither do I know what I will write about from one day to another. This is perhaps one of the hardest ways to write. I pray this journal will be Holy Spirit directed.

Now that you know me, let us better continue. For a long time, I was struggling with the concept of conversational communion with

Jesus. Nearly everyone has prayed the one-sided prayer. We talk to Jesus or Our Father in heaven. We ask Him to forgive us of our sins. We make our request known to Him. There are times when we thank Him for all the blessings that He has given us, but when do we listen? Will Jesus talk back to us? I can assure you here and now, today, that He will! He is ever sending messages to us if we know Him and listen for His voice. James admonishes us to listen in chapter 1:19, "*My dear brothers and sisters, be quick to listen, slow to speak, and slow to get angry.* Psalm 95:6-7 (NLT) "*Come, let us worship and bow down. Let us kneel before the Lord our maker, for he is our God. We are the people he watches over, the sheep under his care. Oh, that you would listen to his voice today!* John 10:14-16 "*I am the good shepherd; I know my own sheep, and they know me, just as my Father knows me and I know the Father. And I lay down my life for the sheep. I have other sheep, too, that are not in this sheepfold. I must bring them also, and they will listen to my voice; and there will be one flock with one shepherd.*" Here are another couple of verses that point out how we can have conversational communion with Jesus. I will again be quoting out of the New Living Translation. Psalm 27:8, "*My heart has heard you say, 'Come and talk with me.' and my heart responds, 'Lord, I am coming.*" Revelation 3:20, "*Look! Here I stand at the door and knock, if you hear me calling and open the door, I will come in, and we will share a meal as friends.*" Now that you know Jesus is always with you, why not talk to Him and listen to what He has to

5

say? Are there questions you would like Jesus to answer? Ask Him and then listen.

You might be asking at this time," How do I isolate the voice of Jesus from all the other voices that are bouncing around in my thoughts?" Have you ever taken the time to listen to your thoughts? Do you always hear a thought voice prattling on and on? Perhaps you have not taken the time to listen to what is going on in your head. When someone ask you a question, do you just answer or does the answer come into your mind first before you speak? Perhaps you have heard someone say, *"think before you speak."* At any given time, there are thought voices going on somewhere in your mind. How can we know which one is the voice of the Good Shepherd? Jesus tells us later in the above chapter John 10:27 (NLT), *"My sheep recognize my voice; I know them, and they follow me."* This indicates there are conditions that must be met before we can hear the voice of Jesus speaking to us. We must be one of the Good Shepherds sheep. To be one of His sheep we must invite Him to be our shepherd or Lord. We know that He is our Savior, but do we make Him our Lord? Are we subservient to His will? When I talk to Jesus, I address Him as Lord.

A few weeks before starting this journal, I was talking to Jesus while planning to do something that was not in His will. I thought I could have Him with me while planning to do something that was not pleasing to Him. He spoke to me very gently, way back in that quiet, upper portion of my mind. "*Why call ye Me Lord, when ye do not the things that I say?*" It was then I realized if I wanted Jesus to walk with me, I needed to obey Him. Jesus tells us, "*If you love Me, keep My commandments.*" John 14:15, (NKJV). Once we determine that a close walk with Jesus is truly what we want more than anything else, Jesus will become our Shepherd and we will know His voice.

How do we know we are in Jesus care and He in us? 1 John 4:13, (NLV). "*And God has given us his Spirit as proof that we live in him and he in us.*" When we are filled with the Spirit of Jesus, He will lead us and guide us. We will hear Him speaking to us personally, directing our way. "*Thine ear shall hear a word behind thee saying, 'This is the way, walk ye in it, when you turn to the right hand and when you turn to the left.*" Isaiah 30:21, (KJV). When we are not in Christ, that guiding voice that we hear could come from a different source. Satan is always at hand to make suggestions. If we yield to his temptations, we will end up committing the sin. So why is it so easy for us to get off track and fall? We find the answer in James 1:14-16, (NLV). Temptation *comes from the lure of our own evil desires. These evil desires lead to evil actions, and evil actions lead to death.* If we are not in Christ, if He is not in control of our will, our desires are not under His influence. Our desires then are not for good, but evil and we open our mind to the suggestions of the evil one.

I just got word that a landscaper I worked for died. After moving to Washington, I did not start my own landscape business right away. I worked for Dave. He was about the same age as I am. I drew up landscape plans for him and oversaw their installation. He always went to Las Vegas before starting his spring, landscape activities. It was a time to take a vacation, rest and have a good time before starting a new year of work. While there his leg started to hurt. He went to the hospital to have it checked out. It was a blood clot. They kept him quiet for a couple of days, but something happened, and the clot moved up and reached his heart. He died there in the hospital. A pain of anguish shot through my heart when I heard about him. It really woke me up. Was he listening to the voice of the Good Shepherd while in Las Vegas? When he took his trip down there, he had no plans to die.

Some of you might be saying to yourself at this time. "This kind of relationship with Jesus sounds really good, Donielle. But I do not know if I even believe in Jesus, or Satan. Where you were raised in a Christian home, I was not. Like the Dave you just mentioned, I never came to a knowledge of Jesus like you. I would like to believe there is a God who loves me and is interested in establishing a friendship with me, but I really do not believe it, at least not down deep inside. What is a person like me who has all of these doubts supposed to do?"

In a passage above the text mentioned: "Taste and see." I would suggest you put Jesus to a test. Either He is who He says He is, or He is not. In Malachi 3, the Lord says. "Prove Me, or test Me." At the time of this writing, we had a gentleman staying with us who was born into a Christian home. He never made a complete commitment to Jesus, however. When he was old enough to not be told what to do by his parents, he decided religion was not for him. He wanted nothing to do with it. Everything was going fine until he lost his job. He tried to find work, but nothing came up. His brother invited him to live with him up on a mountain about 5 miles from a small town. He could build a small house up in the woods and at least survive. So that is what he did. But trouble came. He fell off from the roof of his house and got hurt quite bad. There was no place for him to stay while waiting for a corrective operation on his knee. We took him in. I would try to get into a conversation with him about religious matters, but he would hobble back to the bedroom the first opportunity he had.

One day he lost track of the key to his truck. He spent a long time looking for it without success. When I got home, he told me of his dilemma. I asked if he had prayed about it? Duh? So, I told him that Jesus answers prayer. I shared an experience where I searched for my wallet for a couple of hours. Finally, I prayed and had it in hand half a minute later. I did not know this, but he retired to his room and spoke

"God! Would you help me find my keys?" I was in another room and that little voice of Jesus came to me and said:

"Donielle, look on the key rack for Joe's keys."
I was listening and heard the voice in my mind.
It appeared to be from Jesus, so I walked over to
the key rack and there were the keys. I took them
toward his room and said, "Joe, here are your
keys," He replied.

"I don't believe it! I just prayed 'God!
Would you help me find my keys?' and you said
here are your keys.'"

So put God to the test over the next 30 days.
You could give Him that much time, couldn't you?
He may not answer your prayer as quickly and
as dramatically as that of Joe's, but He does hear
your prayer and will answer. Some of the things
we pray for might not be in our best interest so
He might give a different answer than expected.
But test Him out. See what answers come?

Once you decide to experience
conversational communion with Jesus on an
hourly or moment by moment basis, the enemy
will try everything in his power to keep you from
it. You will need to be on guard. It takes twenty
to thirty days to form a habit. That is why I have
entitled this diary '*30 Days with Jesus.*' I invite
you to take this journey with Jesus and I over the
next 30 days. You can read one day at a time if
you like. This will help form that daily habit of
walking with Jesus. Once the habit is formed it
will be easier to share unbroken communion with
your Lord and mine. At this point, I am eager to
see where Jesus will lead us.

Psalm 34:8

*"O taste and see that the Lord is good: Blessed
is the man that trusteth in Him."*

Day Two

How did your first day with Jesus go? Were you able to isolate His voice from the others? I would like to share a little about the mind with you. It truly is a marvelous organ. A few decades ago, the science world came to understand there is a conscious and subconscious mind. The two orders of mind are in constant communication with each other. Images enter the mind through various senses of sight, touch, smell, taste, and hearing. The brain at any given second is processing hundreds of pieces of information. It catalogues them with other similar perceptions. There is what I call a gatekeeper between the conscious and subconscious mind. When Jesus talks to us, the gatekeeper hears every word that our Lord has to say. He compares the messages Jesus gives us with what is stored in the mind. If what Jesus is saying is totally different than what is in our mind, the gatekeeper might keep a lot of what is said from reaching our consciousness. He is trying to make the conscious mind's work as easy as possible. So, Jesus may be speaking to you, but you might never hear what He has to say. If a person is well versed in the Bible though, the words of Jesus are more likely to reach your conscious thought process. Why? Because the conversational words of Jesus will agree with His words that were written in your mind as you read the Bible.

If you were not able to enter right away into a conversational mode with Jesus, do not be discouraged. You may need to have your conscious mind trained to distinguish His voice. One way to start this education is to read from the Bible in the morning before you begin your work. "*Faith cometh by hearing and hearing from the word of God.*" Romans 10:17 (NKJV) Paul tells us that our conscience can be defiled. Titus 1:15, (NLT) states, "*Everything is pure to those whose hearts are pure. But nothing is pure to those who are corrupt and unbelieving because their minds and consciences are defiled.* If we do not have the faith that comes from reading the Word of God, we are among the unbelievers and our conscious mind is likely to be defiled. It will need to be purified. We are not able to do this of our own. Jesus will have to do this work for us because He only is pure. Therefore, it is necessary to make a complete surrender to Jesus. He cannot do His best work in us until we do this. The process is described in Hebrews 10:22, (NLT) "*Let us go right into the presence of God, with true hearts fully trusting him. For our evil consciences have been sprinkled with Christ's blood to make us clean, and our bodies have been washed with pure water.*" We can enter the presence of Jesus because we have a conscience that has been purified. He made the process possible when He took our sins to the cross. It becomes a reality when we accept His righteousness.

It is important that we do not deliberately sin or fight against the Spirit of Jesus that has begun its work in us. In 1 Timothy 1:19, (NLT) we read, *"Cling tightly to your faith in Christ, and always keep your conscience clear. For some people have deliberately violated their consciences; as a result, their faith has been shipwrecked.* Sin separates us from Jesus. We cannot keep switching back and forth between sin and righteousness and expect to grow up in Christ Jesus. Psalm 66:18, (NLT) states, *"If I had not confessed the sin in my heart, my Lord would not have listened."* Hopefully, everything is right between you and Jesus. If so, then you should be able to deepen your special friendship with Him.

I would like to give a word of caution for you as you seek to hear the voice of Jesus. I have had conversations with a voice in my mind that I imagine to be Jesus. I ask Him questions and receive answers. Nearly anytime I ask a question, an answer comes. Is this thought voice the actual voice of Jesus? Probably not. I like to think it is, but I believe it is the voice of the gatekeeper or that spiritual part of the mind which we refer to as the conscience. Is the conscience answering the way Jesus would answer? Again, probably not. It is answering the way it thinks you would think Jesus would answer. Can I depend on what is being said? For the most part, especially if the question deals with a Biblical topic. Over the years, millions of pieces of spiritual information have entered my mind through several different sources. These have been stored in the recesses of my subconscious. When I need to know some spiritual fact, the thoughts that come from the questions are probably true or close to it. We should not treat them as Gospel Truth though. There is a difference. Holy Men of God spoke or wrote as they were moved by the Holy Spirit. The thought voices you hear may not be the Holy Spirit so do not treat them with the same faith as you place in the Word of God. As we progress in this journal, there will be conversations between me and My Lord. Since my mind is not perfect and I am not one of the Holy Men of old, the conversations should not be regarded as Bible Truth. Most of them will have passed through the gatekeeper or interpreter who put its own interpretation on them.

I have heard the voice of Jesus through the person of the Holy Spirit speaking to my soul many times, which everyone has experience during their life. Most of the time, you probably did not consciously focus on it though and say this is from God. We are told that the Holy Spirit can teach us more in a moment than all the learned men in history. Quite often when inspiration comes, it comes in lump form. The Holy Spirit will plant a great deal of information in your mind in a single moment. After it is there, the conscious mind as well as the subconscious mind go to work on the information to break it down so it can be understood. You have probably had thoughts pop into your conscious mind apparently out of nowhere. These entered the deeper recesses of your mind at some earlier date and surface occasionally as they are deciphered. In your personal communication with Jesus, He will often draw from those resources to get a message across to you.

You may be asking now if conversations between you and Jesus are not actual conversations with the person of Jesus, is its worthwhile pursuing this type of communication? Yes, by all means! If you consider your conversation with Jesus a form of prayer, and are directing your thoughts and communion to Him, your mind is being stayed on Him and the things that are above. The more you are in touch with Jesus and things above, the more intimately acquainted you will become with the One you are placing your affections on. This turning to Christ moment by moment is the goal each of us should strive for. In time, His voice will become clearer, the love He imparts will become stronger, and your friendship with Him deeper. If you have turned your life over to Him, He will use your conversational communion to reveal His will for you. His messages will get through and you will experience the joy of His presence. At some point in your relationship with Christ, you will be walking with Him even as Enoch walked. By beholding Him, you will become changed into His image.

Today was a good day for me. I spent a couple of hours in the morning with my Bible and some devotional reading. I discussed what I read with Jesus. I did not want to leave this time with Him, but He let me know there was occupational work that had to be done today. I was assured of His continuing presence while carrying out my work. We talked about unbroken communion. From His earliest years, Jesus maintained unbroken communion with the Father. On the cross, when Jesus became sin for us, the Father turned His back on His Son. For the first time in His life, Jesus felt the communion that had flowed freely from His Father cut off. It drew from Him the wrenching cry. "*My God, my God, why hast thou forsaken me?*" Matthew 27:46, (KJV). Did you know that you can experience unbroken communion with Jesus? You have heard this text in 1 Thessalonians 5:17, "*Pray without ceasing.*" It is possible to do that. Jesus did it and His life was a testimony to the fact. We can too if we truly know what prayer is. I requested a "how to" from Jesus. I was pointed to the illustration of the branch abiding in the vine. If you cut a branch off from a tree, it will die. The sap that flows freely between the two is cut off. I ask Jesus what the sap represented. It is the Holy Spirit. There is a structural portion of the branch and the vine. In real life it is the cellular tissue and bark. From a spiritual point of view, this physical structure is the breath of life. If there is life, this structure will remain. In winter, when the vine and branches are barren, no sap is flowing between the two. So, in our spiritual life when we are not guided by the Spirit, our Christian life is barren.

The secret to unbroken communion did not fully come until this evening though when I set down to type out these words. I misunderstood what it meant to pray without ceasing. True prayer is two-way communion with Jesus. When things come up, when my conscious mind is engaged in something at hand, the communion flows from Jesus to me. If I still have Jesus within, He is inside working to remove those impure things I have in my life. When I turn my conscious thoughts back to Him, the communion goes to Him or if I am listening, from Him to me. It is good when I talk to Jesus with ears willing to listen. The communion is open ended. It goes both ways. When my mind is engaged with a task at hand, He is there guiding my thoughts, words, and actions. We are told if we allow it, He will so identify Himself with our thoughts, minds and aims that when carrying out our activities here on earth, we will be doing His will. He will personally instruct and teach us in the way we should go.

As I closed my morning session with Jesus, I turned over my daily plans to Him. He impressed me to draw up a design for a firm located about two miles from my home. I dropped my plans and followed the lead Jesus gave. After the design and estimate were finished, I called them. The owner is extremely hard to get a hold of. She was there today though and answered the phone. I saw her 15 minutes later. Jesus set everything up. I went there with a contract, I felt was more than they would pay. I was mistaken. They wanted what I had designed installed and quite a bit more. I will be on the drafting board for many more hours. The work will amount to several thousand dollars. Praise God. He fulfills His promise.

Matthew 6:33

"But seek ye first the kingdom of God, and his righteousness; and all these things shall be added unto you."

Day Three

It is day three already. Ten percent of our time is up. Did you find Jesus today? Perhaps we should talk about goals. Just how deep of a friendship do you want to have with Jesus? Desire is an extraordinarily strong motivating factor. Do you desire to be perfectly hid in Him? If you sincerely desire to live as if in the presence of Jesus, to hear His guiding voice moment by moment, to establish a friendship where you can talk as friends, then make your desire known to Him. He has given us several promises we can claim. Here is one in Psalm 10:17, (NLT). *"LORD, you have heard the desire of the humble: you will prepare their heart, you will incline your ear to hear."* Later in Psalm 21:2, (NLY) there is a similar text, *" You have given him his heart's desire, and have not held back the request he asked."* This is one prayer that Jesus will answer. You do not need to wonder if it is in His will. He wants to be our guide, moment by moment. He has been waiting for over 2000 years to find people who will make Him first, best, and last in everything they do. *"I still belong to you; you are holding my right hand. You will keep on guiding me with your counsel, leading me to a glorious destiny. Whom have I in heaven but you? I desire you more than anything on earth.* Psalm 73:23-25 (NLT)

We are privileged to cooperate with Jesus in a work that is far bigger than we understand.

Jesus understands it though. He has a plan for everyone. He has a plan for you and me. Therefore, we need to be open to His instruction. Today we can cooperate with Jesus as He works to create a new humanity. This new humanity is being born of the Spirit. He wants us to be a part of this new order of being- sinners saved by grace and hid in Christ. Earlier I spoke of goals. It is good for us to set goals, but it is even better to follow the goals Jesus has set for us. This is not easy. For a long time, I wanted to make lots of money. I tried to do this in any way I possibly could. I was determined to meet my goal, but Christ had a different plan. Jesus instructs us in different ways. Sometimes He speaks to us. Sometimes He points us to His Word for instruction. He uses our own personal experiences and the experiences of others. I did not listen to any of these. I still wanted to have my own way. One night I had a dream. I was caught up in this desire for wealth and in my dream, I achieved it. I was in a room. On a table were stacks of cash and coins. It was all mine! I was elated. I had finally reached my goal. As I was glorying in my achievement, an earthquake came. The ceiling over the table started to fall. I ran out of the building and saw some of my friends rising to meet Jesus. He had come to take those who were waiting for Him, home. I had been so busy accumulating money; I was not ready. After they were gone, the world around me seemed dark and empty. I went back into the building and looked at my money. It was all mixed with the debris from the ceiling.

After watching it for a while, I could not tell the difference between it and the chunks of plaster around it. A terrible feeling of being lost came over me. Then I woke up. Jesus did not leave me there. As time progresses, I am beginning to see a small portion of the bigger picture. Jesus has this great plan in mind. It is bigger than anything I could have imagined. It is nice to be on His team now. Doing His will is becoming my desire.

I had another good day with Jesus. I was on the road a lot with an associate of mine. We also worked on a small waterfall project. He seemed to think I was spaced out a bit. I was tuning into the guiding voice of Jesus, I wanted Him to direct the day, yet I was required to carry on a conversation with my other friend. I need more practice in doing this. Somehow there must be a way to not appear spaced out, some way to be in Christ while engaged in the occupational business that is at hand. I kept asking Jesus to help. All in all, things went quite smoothly. On several other occasions, I have arrived on the job with missing tools or supplies needed to complete the work. Not today. There were some tools I felt compelled to load on the truck for no apparent reason but as the day progressed, I found out why they were necessary. With the right tools the work was accomplished in less time. Simple impressions like these are becoming more and more common. An individual came to look at the waterfall we were doing. He tried to make a joke. Since my mind was with Jesus, I did not even realize he was joking. The joke was about a lady that had no arms and no legs. For an answer, I told him she could put her hope in Jesus. Was he ever surprised? The joking stopped after that. When our thoughts are hiding in Christ, He naturally comes out in our conversation.

If you do not find in your heart the desire to experience Jesus in a deeper, more personal way, ask Him to give you that desire. The satisfaction of living in the presence of Jesus every moment of every day is something that cannot be described. It must be experienced. This is a soul need our Creator placed in us. Once filled, we are finally home with Him. To gain this experience though, we must start the day with Him.

How many times has Jesus come to you in the early morning hours before your actual rising time and beaconed you to come and talk with Him? There are countless times I can remember this happening. Most of the time I have done what you probably have done on several occasions, looked at the clock, said its to early Lord, if I spend time with you now, I will be so tired today I will never be able to do all my work if I do not get this sleep. Then I roll over and go back to sleep or try or often am not able to go back to sleep so other thoughts creep into my head that have no earthly good. I end up dwelling on them rather than communicating with Jesus. When this happens and I push Jesus away, He often stays away and no matter how desperately I want Him to return, He seems to be out of reach so I just do what I want to do or think I should do without Him. When this happens, the devil has a field day with me. Since I refused the invitation of Jesus, the enemy forces himself upon me and I end up failing miserably.

It is during the early morning session with Jesus that the course of the day is set. If Jesus is placed at the head, He will guide us throughout the day. If we invite Him to be first, He will take His rightful place in our thoughts and actions and we will end up having the blessed privilege of His company. And we will be blessed Do you find it hard to make a place for Jesus in your day? There is a wonderful promise in the Bible that Jesus longs to fulfill. Here it is. *"The Sovereign Lord has given me his words of wisdom, so that I know what to say to all these weary ones. Morning by morning he wakens me and opens my understanding to his will. The Sovereign Lord has spoken to me, and I have listened. I do not rebel or turn away."* Isaiah 50:4-5, (NLT). Perhaps it is too late today to follow this instruction but there is tomorrow. This evening when you retire, ask Jesus to awaken you in the morning. If you really mean it, He will awaken you and if you follow this practice day by day, you will never miss out on your early morning session with Him. There will always be time for Him. He will see to it personally.

Mark 11.24

"Therefore, I say unto you, what things so ever ye desire, when ye pray, believe that ye receive them, and ye shall have them."

Day Four

How did your early morning session with Jesus go today? Did you ask Him in the evening to waken you in the morning? Did you believe He would? If you really meant it, He probably came to you. I do not know what time you are accustomed to rising. I have always loved to sleep in. It seems my mind does not operate properly if I rise before 6 am. But when Jesus wakes me, it can be as early as 3:30 or 4 am. This was when Jesus arose while He sojourned here on earth. *"And in the morning, rising up a great while before day, he went out, and departed into a solitary place, and there prayed."* Mark 1:35, (NLT). I found that if I were to spend time with Jesus early in the morning, it was good to retire early. The old cliché, "Early to bed and early to rise, makes a man healthy, wealthy and wise" comes to mind. The wisdom portion of this is true if we allow Jesus to commune with us in the morning. We gain in spiritual health and spiritual wealth also.

What should you talk about with Jesus in your early morning sessions? How can anyone spend 1 ½ - 2 hours with Him day after day and not get repetitive? There is a course of worship to follow that will assure each one, hundreds even thousands of productive hours with Jesus in these morning sessions. After Jesus wakes you and the cobwebs of sleep are cleaned from your mind, it is good to start by praising Him. If you do not know how to praise Jesus, go to the Psalms. David and the other authors of those were able to find ways to praise God in every situation we could possibly find ourselves in. If you cannot think of a way to praise God in the morning, open your Bible to some of the Psalms and pray the praise. Seek to put praise for Christ ahead of your own needs and concerns. Focus on His goodness, His mercy, His salvation, His love, His protection, His guidance, His character, His words, and actions while He walked the dusty streets of planet earth.

Next comes confession. When we see how pure and lovely Jesus is, then compare His life with our own, we see there are many ways we fall short of His example. As we turn our thoughts toward our own deficiencies, Jesus will point out areas in our life that need to be surrendered to Him. As He points out these areas, we need to confess them to Him, we need to ask that He give us repentance. We, ourselves are not even able to repent of our sins. It is Jesus who gives us repentance. *"Him hath God exalted with his right hand to be a Prince and a Savior, for to give repentance to Israel, and forgiveness of sins."* Acts 5:31, (KJV). Once He has given us the repentance for our sins, we then ask His forgiveness and open our ears to hear the next area of our life that is not totally surrendered to Him. Jesus will point out some other areas but not all. We would not be able to bear all the areas in one session. To His disciples He once said. *"I have yet many things to say unto you, but ye cannot bear them now.* John 16:12, (KJV). There will be plenty more He will share with us as we allow Him to speak to us morning by morning.

The process of confession is like a mini judgment. God the Father has entrusted all judgment to His Son. As we see the perfect love of Jesus revealed through His sacrifice on the cross, the worse we will appear in our own eyes. As Jesus points out these sinful weaknesses, we need to turn them over to Him. We confess, He forgives, and we move on. In the Christian's judgment, we deal with our sins now. The one who does not deal with their sins now will have to face them in the end and the whole of their sinfulness will be so great, it will destroy them. They will, with their sins be destroyed in the light or fire of God's glory. Sin cannot stand in the presence of a Holy God. So, in the final judgment of the wicked, sin will be burned up along with those who have chosen to hold unto it rather than confess it and give it up to Jesus who paid the penalty for it with His own life.

At this time, it would probably be good to get into the Word of God for a while. We are wide awake. We have given Jesus first place in our thoughts; He has prepared our hearts through repentance. Now we can turn to the Words of life for instruction. Some may want to follow a specific study plan. Perhaps you would like to read your Bible from cover to cover. What I like to do is focus on those text that cover the areas of my life that Jesus just pointed out where I have need to surrender completely to Him. I have a CD with Bible translations all recorded. I take some of the key thoughts that have been pointed out during our session together, put those words in the query, and all kinds of text pops up. As I dwell on those portions of the Scriptures, promises came from the pages of the Bible. These are for me to claim. Most often, these are the words of power I need to transform my life or overcome some specific weakness in my life. Sometimes I pray the Words, making them an offering of myself to God.

As precious promises from God's Word come to me, I put my name in the promise. For example, there is a Bible passage that over half of the people in the United States have heard and would recognize. *"For God so loved the world that he gave his only begotten Son, that whosoever believeth in him should not perish but have everlasting life.* John 3:16. This *passage can be personalized to read something like this: For God loved me, Donielle so much that He sent Jesus into this world so that by choosing to believe in Him, Donielle will not perish but have everlasting life. For God did not send Jesus into the world to condemn me but save me.* John 3:16, 17

I can take that promise from the Bible and place it in my mind along with other passages of Scripture. If I put that personalized promise in that place in my mind where the voice of Jesus comes into my conscious thought, that will be the same voice the Good Shepherd uses when He talks to me, Jesus becomes very personal that way. The Bible becomes His voice to my soul.

To complete this process and make this promise my own I would add. "Thank You, Jesus for this wonderful promise! I do believe in You, I really do. Thank you for giving me this wonderful assurance of living forever with you. Thank You for not coming into this world to condemn, Donielle. You did not come to condemn me but save me. If I ever hear a voice in my mind accusing me or condemning me, saying that I am too bad to be saved in Your kingdom, I will know that is not Your voice speaking to me but the voice of the evil one. *"And I heard a great voice saying in Heaven, 'Now has come the salvation and power and kingdom of our God, and the authority of His Christ. For the accuser of our brothers - the one who accuses me, Donielle, - is cast down, who accused them before our God day and night.'"* Revelation 12:10 (NKJV) Personalized!

Next, I bring my needs to Jesus. He knows all about them already, but it helps to talk to Him about them. I often find after the exercise of other things; my needs seem small and insignificant in comparison to the bigger picture. Lastly, during this time of turning again to Jesus in prayer, I lay out my plans for the day and allow Jesus the opportunity to modify them according to His will and purpose. If you will follow these steps each morning before going about your daily work, Jesus will do His wonderful work in you and you will find yourself on a path to a glorious relationship with your Lord and Savior, Jesus Christ. Your life will have a purpose that goes beyond your grandest expectations. *"The way of the righteous is like the first gleam of dawn, which shines ever brighter until the full light of day"*, Proverbs 4:18 This first gleam of dawn or some versions call it a path that leads to the Light. Have you ever looked in a mirror in a darkened room? A lot of the blemishes you have are hidden in the darkness. Now take that same mirror out into the sunshine and investigate it and every blemish, every imperfection becomes noticeably clear. So, it is as we enter the perfect light of Jesus that the blemishes and dark spots in our character becomes noticeably clear to us. As they are pointed out, we must abandon them through the power Jesus imparts through His love.

It was one of those beautiful spring days today. I was outside a lot, especially in the afternoon. Today as I invited Jesus into my heart, I felt Him working inside of me, changing my life little by little. There was a softening of my character. The rough edges were being smoothed out by the hands of the Carpenter. I have been consciously connecting with Him more and more as the day progresses. I am not totally in the habit yet but am getting closer. There was something about the warm sun on my shoulders, the gentle breezes that reminded me of being touched by my Creator. It was a soft, gentle, loving touch. I could sense His arm around me at times and the deep love He has for me. I cannot understand that kind of love. Only a Creator can have that kind of love for His child, but it is wonderful to be there. A song came to my mind as I was working. It is one of the best beloved hymns of all time, *"In The Garden."*

I come to the garden alone, while the dew is
still on the roses.
And the voice I hear, falling on my ear, The
Son of God discloses.
And He walks with me, and He talks with me.
And He tells me I am His own.
And the joy we share as we tarry there, none
other has ever known.

He speaks and the sound of His voice, is so
sweet the birds hush their singing.
And the melody that He gave to me within
my heart is ringing.
And He walks with me, and He talks with me.
And He tells me I am His own.
And the joy we share as we tarry there, none
other has ever known.

I'd stay in the garden with Him, though the
night around me be falling.
But He bids me go; through the voice of woe,

His voice to me is calling.
And He walks with me, and He talks with me.
And He tells me I am His own.
And the joy we share as we tarry there, none
other has ever known.

I never realized it before, but the author of this song stayed in the garden with Jesus all day long. Jesus walked with him and talked with him and told him he was his own. He speaks of joy that none other has ever known. That is what it is like with Jesus. "*Thou wilt show me the path of life: in thy presence is fulness of joy; at thy right hand there are pleasures for evermore.*" Psalm 16.11, (KJV). Jesus will show us the right path to take in our life. He also tells us we are His own. "*But now thus saith the LORD that created thee, O Jacob, and he that formed thee, O Israel, Fear not: for I have redeemed thee, I have called thee by thy name; thou art mine.*" Isaiah 43:1, (KJV). As the song died away in my mind the sun was setting. I went back to the design table and worked late but the joy of the day, the personal closeness with Jesus was wonderful. Ask Jesus to give you a song today. Let it be playing in the background of your mind as you go about your daily task. Some thoughts may interrupt it at times, but it will return again and again to bring comfort, or hope, or blessing. If Jesus chooses the song for you, it will be just what you need for the day. It is a nice way to stay connected with your Lord. At times I have carried a little hymnal with me and throughout the day have committed the words of a song to memory. You can also do this with scripture cards.

Psalm 40:3

"He put a new song in my mouth, a hymn of praise to our God.

Day Five

It snowed today. It is hard to believe the weather can change so quickly. Last evening, I was up late and got up early to get some things done that were on my list. I did not take the time to meet with my Lord as I had on the four previous days. As the day advanced, I could sense the lack of His presence more and more. I had an appointment to take our dog to town to get her stitches out. There was one problem though, I could not find my keys. Thinking back to a time when a friend of mine had a direct answer to prayer in finding his keys, I did not wait long before praying. After checking my pockets, the key rack, and the truck without success, I prayed. As I paused to listen a little voice came quietly to my mind.

"The keys are in your jacked pocket, Donielle." I had already checked my jacket pocket and there were no keys. So, I went and checked again. I secretly wondered if perchance there was a hole in one of the pockets and the keys slipped down to the hem? Nope! There was nothing in any pocket. So, I turned again to the lovely Jesus.

"Jesus. I did not find them in any of my jacket pockets."

"The keys are in the other jacket pocket, Donielle." The jacket I remember wearing before was hanging on a peg in the garage so off I went.

Again, I was disappointed. The keys were not in that jacket either. I tried to go over in my mind what could be the problem? I knew that my Lord had given me awfully specific instructions and always before they had proved to be right.

"You visited the pastor," the voice came again. Time was running out. The appointment was coming. Joe was getting ready to go to town. I could catch a ride with him. He loved dogs; he would not have a problem bringing her along. You see, Joe is the one who had lost his keys just a couple of weeks earlier and when I suggested he pray, he acted like I was kidding. When I prayed, I had been told his keys were on the key rack so going into his room, I had told him here were his keys. At that time, he said to me.

"I just prayed and asked God. 'Help me find my keys,' and you came into the room right after.

"Joe, here are your keys." So, I had this wonderful opportunity to help a former Christian pray again and seek a God he had rejected. Even though Joe had abandoned God, God had not abandoned him and had answered his prayer in a miraculous way.

The enemy of my soul was taunting me.

"Donielle? You are out of time. Prayer did not work. Go ask Joe to give you and the dog a ride into town. You can tell him you lost your keys." I should know by now to listen carefully to the voices that come into my mind. This one did not sound right so I paused. This voice was too hurried, almost sarcastic. Suppose I had followed his suggestion? The conversation would have gone something like this.

"Joe?"

"Yes, Donielle."

"Do you remember losing your keys the other day?"

"How could I forget?"

"Well, I misplaced my keys. I prayed and looked and looked and have not been able to find them. I must get this dog to town by 9am to get her stitches out. Could you give us a ride?

How would a conversation like that effect the small amount of faith that was sprouting up in the heart of Joe? It would most likely crush it. The enemy would have gained a victory. The voice of the enemy came more urgently this time. It was overpowering.

"You better hurry, Donielle, Joe is about to leave! On the way to town, you guys can have a good laugh about answered or unanswered prayer. It will be fun! Sometimes it works, sometimes it doesn't."

Before I go further with this story, compare the impressions or voice thoughts from Jesus with those from the enemy. You have heard both rivals battling back and forth in your mind time and again. Do you recognize the difference? If you filter these thought impressions through the Word of God, it will help you separate the true from the false. You will be able to discern the voice of the righteous One from that of the wicked one. So often we do not try to discern who is making those suggestions to us.

I prayed one more time, a little more desperately this time as I started walking. I ran across the coveralls I had used while crawling around in the crawl space beneath the house a few days earlier. Could the keys be under the house in that crawl space? When I bent to lift the cover, I saw another jacket. Instantly I remembered. That was the nice jacket, the one I use when going to appointments. That was the jacket I had on when I visited the pastor. I reached into the pocket and there were the keys. Jesus had to run me through a series of exercises to help me remember where the keys were. His answers to my prayer were right on. What more could He do?

The enemy had tried to make the prayer into defeat. He tried to knock my faith into the ground and discourage Joe in the same temptation. Jesus does not leave us to our own devices if we place a little faith and trust in Him. He came to the rescue and turned that defeat into victory. I wonder if this day would have started out better had I not neglected to turn to my Lord upon awakening. Perhaps realizing that I was going to take the dog in, He would have reminded me to use the nicer jacket, the one I use when I go to meet people. Had this been the case, I would have reached into my pocket and found the keys? Who knows how it would have worked out?

Our common enemy does not like to see us becoming too familiar with Jesus. What does Jesus do with us during these colder days, when the winds blow, and the snow obliterates our vision of the Sun of Righteousness? He prays for us. How comforting it is to know that. His prayer is effective also because His Word says: *"The effectual fervent prayer of a righteous man availeth much."* James 5:16, (KJV). Jesus is righteous. He is righteousness personified. He is the Sun of Righteousness so His prayers for us are highly effective. What else can He do? If I have not actively invited Him to share in my life, He can only do a little of what He wants to do in me. So, He prays for me. *"Neither pray I for these alone, but for them also which shall believe on me through their word; That they all may be one; as thou, Father, art in me, and I in thee."* John 17:20-21, (KJV). We still belong to Jesus. The Father has given us to Him. He still claims us and prays for the time when we will again be one with Him, just as He is one with the Father. Jesus also invites the Holy Spirit to come to work in our life. *"And I will ask the Father, and He will give you another Counselor, who will never leave you. He is the Holy Spirit, who leads into all truth. The world at large cannot receive him, because it is not looking for him and does not recognize him. But you do because He lives with you now and later will be in you. No, I will not abandon you as orphans–I will come to you.*" John 16:16-18 (NLT).

The Holy Spirit also prays for us. "*And the Holy Spirit helps us in our distress. For we do not even know what we should pray for, nor how we should pray. But the Holy Spirit prays for us with groanings that cannot be expressed in words.*" Romans 8:26 (NLT). In the Gospel of John, it is interesting to note that none of the Trinity do anything of their own accord. Jesus does what the Father tells Him to, and the Father takes council in His Son. The Holy Spirit does what the Son wishes and all three are one. It is their desire that we be one with them. The God we place our belief in lives to serve. That is what we are to do on earth. We are placed here to serve one another and by doing that we glorify the Father. Heaven will be a wonderful place. Everyone will be doing their best to serve others, and each will find that they cannot out give the Lord because for everyone they serve, they will be served ten times or more.

After I completed the work on my business, I remembered to invite my Lord into my heart. For the next few hours, He kept me busy, instructing me how to serve those immediately around me. There were several household chores that He pointed out that would lighten the load of my wife. When we are walking with Jesus, even these task that in the past have seemed bothersome, becomes a joy because we have

His companionship. Even the prison cell can become a place of Glory with the presence of Jesus. I look forward to a bright, new day with Him, tomorrow. It is a special day, the Sabbath. On this day above all others, He longs to enter fellowship with us.

Luke 22:31-32

"Simon, Simon, Satan has desired to have you, that he may sift you like wheat. But I have prayed for you, that your faith fails not."

Day Six

It was a good day with Jesus today. I went to church and told the children's story. I had a nice talk with my sister over the phone. There was some good food at lunch. But the evening was the best. It is quiet in the house now. I am here alone with my thoughts and with Jesus. There is another being here also from the courts of heaven. He is my guardian angel. He and Jesus are well acquainted with each other. They go back ages before this world was ever created. Both were here when Jesus–the Word–spoke this world into existence. Both know me better than I know myself. They talk with each other quite often and they talk about me a lot. They cooperate to lead me as far as I will allow them in fulfilling the plans Jesus has laid out for me. Both have been on hand to save me from certain destruction. There were a thousand paths I started down, but they stood in the way and arranged circumstances that turned me from the darkness to the light. Before I was born Jesus sat down with my guardian angel and laid out the plan He had for my life. I am sure angels have names. I inquired once as to the name of my guardian angel and the word Rashahanna came to mind. Whether that is his name or not I will not really know until I can ask him on that glorious white cloud that is heaven bound at our Lord's return. But let us assume his name is Rashahanna. On or around the time I was expected to make my entrance into this world, Jesus and Rashahanna got together. Jesus started the conversation.

"Donielle will soon be born, Rashahanna. Here is the plan I have laid out for his life. Your work is to see that it is followed as closely as possible. If you ever see anything coming that will prevent this plan from being fulfilled, if anyone or anything gets in the way, I want you to intervene. I am giving you all of the power you need to see that this plan is met." As the two of them talked on and on, Jesus laid everything out for this angel. As I grew and developed, Rashahanna did exactly what Jesus asked him to do. He has been there from day one to the present. How many times has he spared my life? How many temptations has he helped me avert, temptations that would have sunk me deep into the pit of sin? How many plans have I made for myself that he has changed because they did not measure up to the plan of Jesus? Again, I will not know this until I ask him when this corruptible will put on incorruption and this mortal will be given immortality. On that day, the glory of Jesus that has been working within will be completed and I will be transformed to that glorified state that will allow me to enter the presence of the Father. Jesus has a plan for my life, and He has a plan for yours. *"'For I know the plans I have for you,' declares the Lord, "'plans to prosper you and not to harm you, plans to give you hope and a future. Then you will call upon me and come and pray to me, and I will listen to you. You will seek me and find me when you seek me with all your heart. I will be found by you,"' declares the Lord.* Jeremiah 29:11-14 (NIV).

There is so much in this Scripture that speaks to me. Could there be any better plans for my life than the ones my Creator has made for me? Are His plans for me the ones that cause me to be miserable? Is the Christian life He wants me to follow a burdensome one? No! He has plans to prosper me physically, mentally, spiritually, and emotionally. He does not have plans to harm me, but better yet, He wishes to remove the tendencies I have towards sin. He has a glorious, bright future planned for me that is full of hope. He wants me to come to the place in my life where we talk as friends. When I call upon Him, He will listen and respond. I am assured that I will find Him when I seek for Him with all my heart. If I determine to do all in my power to do nothing that will displease Him, I will find Him. Then to seal it all up, He signs it with His signature; "For I declare it," says the Lord. Why, O why have I been so slow to enter His plans? What might have happened in my life had I been more willing to be in friendship with Jesus—day by day, moment by moment? What truths has He been longing to share with me, anxiously waiting for the time when I will offer Him all my heart? And what about the angel companion that is right beside Him, ready to cooperate in every way to complete this work in my life?

In Matthew 18:10, (Living Bible) we read these words. *"Beware that you don't look down upon one of these little children. For I tell you that in heaven their angels have constant access to my Father."* How does it make you feel to know that you are never alone? At any moment you have at your side a mighty angel who ever has access to the courts of heaven. His sole purpose in life is to see that you are following the plan Jesus has laid out for your life. Do you know when you are the happiest? It is when you are following the plans of Jesus. If you do not find yourself happy now, turn to your Lord. He is present with you this very moment. Tell Him what is on your heart. You could pray a prayer like this:

"Dear Jesus. I know that If You have a plan for my life because Your Word tells me that you do. It is an incredibly detailed plan. You have a plan for me today. I do not know what that plan is. I set these plans for myself. I plan to _____. But Jesus, my plan for this day may not be the same as your plan for me. You have something You want me to do today. Have Your way in my life. I know the plans that you have laid out for me are plans that would make me the happiest person on earth were I to follow them. You made me. You know me. You gave me special characteristics and talents that were especially made for the plans You have for me. I do not feel I am following your plans very well.

If I am not, Jesus, please tell me what to do. I want to be in your will. You have promised in James 1:5, if I ask, you will give me wisdom. And I ask that you present me with that wisdom now so I can fulfill the work You have appointed for me today. You have also assured me all power is available for me to carry out the tasks You want me to do. There is also a mighty angel who is with me, pledged to help carry out Your work. There is nothing the enemy can send to prevent this plan from being fulfilled so long as I remain in You. Have Your way in my life today. I ask this in your wonderful name, Jesus, that name that means for 'He shall save His people from their sins. Amen."

As I look back on my life, there were several times that things happened through Divine intervention. I will share one experience with you now. I was doing my student teaching at a public high school. On this day, I felt I was all alone in the room with a group of kids who were under the control of Satan. They were not doing their work. They did not plan to do it. They knew I had little power to make them do what they were supposed to, and they were having what they considered to be a great time. It was later in the year when their regular teacher was enjoying his hour off in the teachers' lounge. This sense of a dark power present in the room overwhelmed me. I did not know what to do so I begin to pray. I turned my face a little so the students could not see that I closed my eyes. In my mind, I lifted each one of the students up to heaven. I appealed to each of their guardian angels to prevail and push back the suffocating powers of darkness. To make this prayer more dramatic, before starting it, a dark cloud outside had blocked the sun. When I finished appealing to the last of the angels–who ever have access to the Father–the dark cloud outside vanished. Brilliant rays of sunshine poured in through the windows and united with the glory of the guardian angels stationed around each student. With one united effort they prevailed against the evil angels who were also present in the room. The transformation was one of the most amazing events I have witnessed. The students suddenly lost interest in their devilry. It was a class in mechanical drawing. Those who were not at their boards returned to them. They got out their pencils and went to work. Since it was a drawing class, their regular teacher allowed them to talk if they kept it down. The conversation changed to one of a spiritual nature. I was praising God. To me it was a miracle of the power of angels.

There was one red haired student who had been one of the main instigators of the discipline problems I was experiencing. I noticed him especially as the calm came over the room. In that peaceful environment–where the glory of God was being passed around–he was extremely uncomfortable. I believe the enemy had come to control him nearly completely. He could not settle down so he came up to my desk and made a statement I will never forget. It was one that wrenched my heart.

"I know where I'm going, Mr. Ingersoll. I'm going straight to Hell." I prayed awfully hard at that point. I again petitioned all the guardian angels present to join to help him with this struggle he was experiencing. His face relaxed and over the next several minutes I talked to him about hope that we can have when we are on God's side. In your walk with Jesus, know that there are two powerful beings who ever have access to the courts of heaven. You are never far from help. There may be legions of evil angels trying to prevent you from carrying out the plans Jesus has for you. But if you will appeal to your guardian angel, and your constant companion, Jesus Christ, there is nothing that can prevent His work from being carried out. One guardian angel–filled with the glory radiating from the throne of the Father–can dispel any dark clouds of evil that are surrounding you. All the power of heaven is at your disposal. Do not give up. Do not lose hope. Jesus is mighty to save, and He loves you more than you can ever possibly understand.

At this point I need to give a warning. In your search for the perfect walk with Jesus stay away from all forms of altered consciousness. By altered consciousness I mean attempting through relaxation exercises or self-hypnosis to attain an altered state of mind. There are several churches that offer instruction in Contemplative Prayer or other names for communion methods that require the person to go through a relaxation or meditation process. They typically have a person through breathing and relaxation exercises to consciously enter a slowed down state of brain wave activity before seeking some higher power. Stay Away From All Forms Of This Type Of Prayer Or Worship. Our common enemy the Devil, and Satan dominates these methods. If you venture onto his ground in these areas, you will give him the key to your mind and soul. He will come in and attempt to destroy you and any faith you have in Jesus. Please, I cannot stress this enough. Stay away from all types of self-hypnosis! Do not practice any form of channeling otherworldly entities. Evil spirits are waiting and all too eager to communicate with you through these means.

Hebrews 1:14

"Are they (the angels) not all ministering spirits, sent forth to minister for them who shall be heirs of salvation?"

Day Seven

This is day seven. We have spent one week in the presence of Jesus. Take a few minutes and evaluate your spiritual walk this last week. Do you feel closer to Jesus than you were a week ago? Have you allowed Him to wake you morning by morning? Has He become a more real and present part of your life? How often have you heard His voice speaking to you? How have your plans changed? Were there some things He impressed you to do? If so, did you do them? If you did them, how do you feel about what happened? Do you fall to sleep with Him on your thoughts at night? Do you wake up each morning to the sunshine of His grace? Have you felt His presence near you or within you? If you have, where was He? When I sense the presence of Jesus, He is behind me next to my right shoulder. He is taller than I am. I must look up to see Him with my mind's eye. His voice comes to the upper right-hand portion of my mind somewhere above my right ear. His voice is soft and melodious. Sometimes, His words come with an urgent tone. Sometimes, there is a hint of a suggestion. At times, comfort flows so sweet from Him, I am melted by His love and can hardly contain the joy within. When I ask

Him a question or am about to ask the question, I often have the answer even before I phrase the question. I went to the Bible to see if my perceptions of Him are correct. Here is a Bible text from Psalms. David had one of the closest walks with Jesus of any Bible character while he was humble. He was greatly loved by Jesus and one of the great kings of all time. Here is what He says. *"I bless the Lord who gives me counsel; in the night also, my heart instructs me. I keep the Lord always before me; because he is at my right hand, I shall not be moved. Therefore, my heart is glad, and my soul rejoices; my body also dwells secure."* (Psalm 16:7-9 (RSV)

Jesus is at the Psalmist right hand in this passage of Scripture and He is also at your right hand. Earlier in one of our Bible texts, we read where our ear will hear a word behind us saying, "This is the way, walk in it." So, a word from behind and at the right-hand side. That is where Jesus appears to be. About the answers that come before the question, is there support in the Bible for this? *"And it shall come to pass, that before they call, I will answer; and while they are yet speaking, I will hear."* Isaiah 65:24, (NIV). There are times when my heart speaks to me also. At times in the past, I have come to a point in my life where my prayer to Jesus has been a soul cry from my heart. When some trial came that seemed too severe, when some prayer I had trusted Him for an answer to, never happened, at times like these,

I have prostrated myself on the floor and cried out to God. With my body tensed and my fingers digging into the strands of carpet, my heart has prayed to God. A stream of anguish too great to express in conscious words has flowed up to heaven. And in those desperate times, a stream has flowed back from the courts of glory. It has surged in and washed my soul clean. In the end, a peace comes that passes my understanding. This is soul prayer, the prayer of the heart. Hannah prayed this kind of prayer. "*And it came to pass, as she continued praying before the LORD, that Eli marked her mouth. Now Hannah, she spoke in her heart; only her lips moved, but her voice was not heard therefore, Eli thought she had been drunken.*" 1Samuel 1:12-13. (NIV).

This type of prayer is when the heart is spilled out and broken and the healer of broken hearts comes to mend it. My heart has instructed me after these seasons, for the stream of hope, truth and comfort that flows back is too large for my conscious reason to take in all at once. Over the next several hours it is decoded, and my Instructor goes over it sentence by sentence. At times, the instruction has lasted far into the night and though the darkness is all around, yet it is light within. Understanding comes and I leave that place of prayer with my questions answered.

I like the morning prayer as light comes streaming through the eastern window in our bedroom. I close my eyes and am carried away on the beams of sunshine to a glorious rest with my Redeemer. It is not like this all the time. Sometimes days come and go before a noteworthy response to my prayer happens. At other times, it may come for two or three days together. Everything in this world at those special times loses its appeal and I long for Jesus to come so the experience can last for eternity. At these times, *"I know that my Redeemer lives."* Job 19:25. A person might wonder why after experiencing such a remarkable time like this with Jesus, they would ever doubt, but it happens. Things come up and the spiritual high goes down. Then the darkness comes in like a cloak, shutting out the rays of glory streaming from the throne of grace. Cold winds blow around in my soul and I shiver in the darkness and wonder if there is a way out. Hopelessness binds up my heart with ropes of despair. Is Jesus as present in the times of darkness as He is in those times of light? Yes, He is. Though the warmth of His presence does not seem to have any effect, He is still there. *"For the enemy hath persecuted my soul; he hath smitten my life down to the ground; he hath made me to dwell in darkness, as those that have been long dead. Therefore, is my spirit overwhelmed within me; my heart within me is desolate. I remember the days of old; I meditate on all thy works; I muse on the work of thy hands. I stretch forth my hands unto thee: my soul thirsteth after thee, as a thirsty land. Hear me speedily, O LORD: my spirit faileth: hide not thy face from me, lest I be like unto them that go down into the pit. Cause me to hear thy lovingkindness in the morning; for in thee do I trust cause me to know the way wherein I should walk; for I lift my soul unto thee. Deliver me, O LORD, from mine enemies: I flee unto thee to hide me."* Psalm 143:3-9, (KJV).

Then He comes again like the warmth of that spring day I experienced earlier. Today was another warm day. At first, only a trickle of the Spirit flowed through my drowsy mind. Then as the day progressed, as I leaned more and more on Jesus, He came. He came with His arms of comfort outstretched to hold me. I retreated into them and found His rest. We had a quiet talk while I busied myself with some work outside. One of the tasks was pruning our grapes. The pruning was sever . 80-90% of the branches were removed. In those dark times when it seems the Lord is far away, He is not. He is very nearby. We are receiving the pruning of the Lord. He comes in and removes a large portion of the things in this world that have entwined themselves in our heart. They take up too much of our time thus shutting down our communion with heaven. Once removed the fellowship with Jesus is more focused and more, sweeter. There are fewer distractions, and He can nourish us more completely with His Spirit.

After pruning the grapes, I retired to a place of prayer that we have. In this place, Jesus and I have met on more than one occasion to fellowship, one with another. After a few minutes, I fell asleep talking to Him while His peace washed over me. *"I will not leave you comfortless: I will come to you."* John 14:18, (KJV). If Jesus has not come to you yet, do not despair. Do not give up. Set your hope in Him. Trust His promise. He will come just as He promised because He is truth and cannot lie. *"You shall seek Me and find Me, Son, you shall seek Me and find Me, Daughter; you shall seek Me and find Me, Beloved, when you seek Me with all of your heart."*

Psalm 130:1-2

"O Lord, from the depths of despair I cry to you for help: Hear me! Answer! Help me!"

Day Eight

This is the start of the second week on our Thirty Days with Jesus. I am personally finding that I am more aware of Jesus, more of the time. My thoughts turn to Him a lot more often than they did a week ago. As we continue, I wonder how much more personal He will become? How specific will His conversations with me be? I have heard of others who keep drawing closer and closer. They have had extremely specific conversations. Jesus' instruction to them is understood very clearly. When they follow His bidding, His guidance leaves no room for doubt. I am going to share a couple of these stories with you today.

Back in 1958, Spire Books published a modern rewrite of Brother Lawrence's letters with Spiritual Maxims called, "The Practice of the Presence of God. Brother Lawrence lived in the 1600s. For the last forty years of his life, he learned to live as if in the presence of God every waking moment of every day. His writings have inspired millions. A pastor purchased the book that year and began to follow the instructions in his daily life. He would open the door for Jesus before driving to his appointments every day. When he wrote his sermons, he conversed with Jesus about each part. He came so close to Jesus;

his life was totally transformed. Looking back on his first 30 years of ministry, he understood why one of his sons left the church. He talked to Jesus about all the mistakes he had made and asked for a second chance. But the years came and went with no change. His son never called home. They did not know if he was dead or alive, married, or single. He just stepped out of their lives, forever. In 1970, 12 years after this pastor started walking with Jesus, I attended a church service where he spoke. I was 17 at the time. The church service went a half hour overtime. We did not care. After a fellowship meal, he spoke again. He told story after story detailing where Jesus had led in his life in the most miraculous ways. The following is one I still remember after over 50 years.

One day Pastor Snyder was traveling alone to Chicago. It was about a 3-hour trip from his home. As his habit was before starting, he opened the passenger door for Jesus and invited Him to ride along. While they rode, they conversed as two friends would on a trip. As Chicago loomed closer, the tone of Jesus' voice changed. Pastor Snyder had heard it so often, he was surprised at the difference. Jesus took control of the conversation and when they came to a road that was unfamiliar to the pastor, Jesus told him to turn left. So, the pastor–we will call him Kenneth–turned left. They went several blocks and Jesus told him to turn left again. Then he was instructed to turn right. After a dozen turns, Kenneth started to get a little worried. They were entering a part of Chicago that did not look good. There were abandoned, stripped out, and burned vehicles along the streets. The houses were run down. Garbage was strung all over. Some of the streets were so loaded up it was hard to pass through them. As he turned down one dingy road, he saw four rough looking guys heading toward him. They took up the whole street.

"Shall I keep going, Jesus," he asked?

"Yes, Ken."

"What about these guys who are coming towards me? They don't look like they plan to move out of the way."

"They will part, Ken. Just keep driving." And sure, enough they separated down the middle. As Kenneth looked out the window at them, it was as if they never saw the car. After a few more turns, he started to question the whole thing. Then Jesus instructed them to turn down a dead-end street. At this point the Pastor did argue with his Lord.

"This whole thing is crazy, Jesus," he said. "Now we have a dead-end street and the people here look even less friendly than the four guys we saw earlier."

"Do you trust Me Ken?" Jesus asks.

"Yes, Jesus."

"Have I ever let you down?"

"No."

"Do you trust Me now?"

"Okay, Jesus. You have made your point," he responded. At the end of the dead-end street, Ken spotted a trailer hooked to a pick-up. There was a missing tire on the truck. One headlight was smashed out. The trailer at first sight, looked abandoned. Ken was about to turn around, but Jesus told him to stop and go up to the door. After questioning Jesus one more time, he spoke.

"I will go, but you have to go with me, Jesus." He got out, opened the passenger door for his friend and the two of them went up to the trailer. He knocked and a dark haired, young lady answered. Two small, dirty faced, heads poked out from behind her and looked up at him. The lady spoke.

"May I help you?" Kenneth had never seen her before. "What should he tell her," He asked himself. Should he say, "I was riding with Jesus and he directed me here so here I am?" That would sound too strange. Finally, he responded.

"I saw there was a tire missing on your truck, and I wondered if you needed some help."

"No," she answered. "We are fine. Thanks for inquiring" She started to close the door but from the back of the trailer a young man thought he recognized the voice and came out. Pastor Snyder was simply amazed at what he saw. From that point on he never doubted his Lord's leading again because there at door was the son, he had not seen for seven years. The two looked at each other, speechless for a moment then the son ran and threw his arms around his father.

"Dad! You are here? How did you ever find me?"

"It's a long story, Son. Do you have about two hours?

"More if you need it, Dad."

"Are these your children?"

"Yes, Dad. This is my wife, and these are your grandsons." Kenneth had grandsons he had never seen or known about. Jesus dialed up the love and old wounds were healed. His lost son was found, and Pastor Snyder was given his second chance. This time, Jesus was his daily helper, and the relationship was restored. After hearing of the miraculous trip, his son responded.

"You're different, Dad. Your God is different too. He is real now. If He cares enough about me to send you to a place like this, then I am ready to give Him a try. I am ready to come home."

The second story is equally amazing if not more so. Another pastor who had learned to listen to the voice of Jesus was trying to finish his sermon one morning, when he was told to put it up and go to a nearby hospital to see one of his members. She had been suffering with severe pain for months. Her life was ending. As he paused for a few moments to consider her, he sent up a prayer to heaven. He felt that if he spent a few moments praying for her, that would be enough, and he could get back to his sermon. But Jesus had other plans for the pastor.

"Put your sermon away and go visit, Catherine, John."

"I can't, Lord. I have been working on this sermon all week and I am not getting anywhere. If I go to the hospital, it will never be finished in time for the 11:00 service."

"Go to the hospital, now." By this time, the voice had taken on the form of a command. John knew better than to disobey, so he put his sermon up and left. It took about 20 minutes to get there from his home. When he arrived and went up to her room, he found her surprisingly alert. At other visits she had been so drugged, it was hard to understand what she was saying. Not today, though. She smiled up at him and spoke.

"I was just talking to Jesus and ask Him to send someone to visit me. He sent you, Pastor. About an hour ago I had a visitor. He came into my room and talked with me for over half an hour. I wanted to share this story with someone before they come to give me my medications at 8:00. Jesus came to visit me. I was praying to Him like I always do in the morning and He came into my room. He answered all my questions. For years, there were things I never understood. I have also asked Him to let me go to rest several times over the last few years. I am so glad He waited. I am ready to die now, Pastor. Jesus gave me all the assurance I need. I just had to tell someone. Thank you for coming."

Pastor John had heard of others who claimed to have a similar visit from Jesus a few days before their death. On one occasion, there was a scent of roses in the air. On another, it was as if the air had been cleaned fresh from a spring rain. With this lady though, her face was radiating with glory. He stayed for about half an hour and she told him in detail what Jesus had talked to her about. That pastor would not tell my sister and I what Mother told him in confidence. He assured us; however, she had finally yielded all to Jesus and was ready to go. She had been a worrier all her life. Every little thing seemed to cause her concern. But this time, a peace had come over her that changed her countenance. The enemy knew he had lost this one. She lived for about a week after that visit from Jesus. During that time, Satan handed her more pain than anyone should ever be called to bear, but she never lost hope. She died with the assurance of Salvation from Jesus, Himself.

In the cases of the above three people, Jesus communicated with each in a little different way. Pastor Snyder had tuned his ear to the point where on occasion, Jesus was able to guide him step by step. Another story of him confirmed this. While on a trip in Florida, they stopped to get some oranges at one of the orchards. The owner told them to go and sample the fruit of several trees. When they found a tree that was simply perfect, they could pick their oranges from it. So that is what they did. Pastor had sampled several oranges when he realized that some of his teeth were missing. There was some type of brace that held them in place. He first asked his wife. She laughed.

"We'll just have to stop and visit a dentist that specializes in your type of teeth." Pastor Snyder did not want to do that. It was embarrassing for one thing and probably costly for another. He turned to his Lord for help. Jesus guided him step by step, row by row back to the exact spot where the bracket with his teeth had fallen. We can come to a point in our walk with Jesus, where we too, can hear him guiding us moment by moment in a specific way.

In the case of the second pastor, he was able to recognize the voice of Jesus also but not all the time. Jesus worked on occasion to lead him. He followed the leading, enough to recognize the voice of his Lord. Several of us have received impressions to go somewhere or do something and when we have obeyed, our hearts thrill to realize that Jesus truly has led. The results of our obedience confirm that He was leading in a specific way.

Few are given the same opportunity that Mother experienced. At these special times, Jesus is not just a guiding voice. He comes in person with a special message. The Bible mentions several individuals who were privileged to have a personal visit from Jesus or an angel. They have both heard Him speak and seen Him there with them. Since there are accounts of this on record, we need to understand that if necessary, Jesus will reveal Himself to us in person. *"Those who obey my commandments are the ones who love me. And because they love me, my Father will love them, and I will love them. And I will reveal myself to each one of them."* John 14:21, (NLT). Perhaps you will be one who Jesus chooses to visit personally. Jesus told David to seek His face. If we seek Jesus day by day, moment by moment, if we obey His commandments, He will reveal Himself to each one of us in His own way.

John 14:3

"I go to prepare a place for you, (Catherine), and as surly as I go, I will come again and receive you unto Myself, that where I am, you will be also."

Day Nine

Did you wake up to the presence of Jesus today? If so, how did He wake you? Did He tap you on your shoulder? Did He awaken you through your mind? Did something happen in your house or outside that woke you to the realization that Jesus was there, waiting? Perhaps your telephone rang. Yesterday we talked about having a personal visit from Jesus. Suppose that your telephone rang, and Jesus was on the other end of the line. The call would go something like this.

"Hello, Donielle, this is Jesus. I called to let you know I will be coming to visit you for a week. I will be arriving in about an hour." What would you do? How would you spend the next hour? Would you go through your house and get rid of some things? Would you change your schedule? Would you throw away some books? Would you get out your Bible and dust it off perhaps? What about the food you have? Would you need to go shopping to get the proper food for such an influential person? If Jesus were to pay you a visit today, how would your day change?

In the morning, He would get up at 3 or 4 am and find a quiet spot to talk with His Father. He would probably get back to your home a little before 6. Would you spend a few minutes in family worship with Him? You would need to have some breakfast for Him. It would not be polite to not talk with Him, would it? What would your conversation at the breakfast table be if Jesus were filling one of the chairs? After breakfast, while you are preparing to go to work, you would have occasion to talk with Jesus. What would you talk about then? Would you invite Him to help you plan out your schedule for the day? If you must drive to work, what would you talk about with Jesus as you were traveling? Then at work, He would be by your side all day long. Would you talk to Him throughout the day? What would you talk about? If some of your associates at work were to ask you what you were thinking about, would you talk to them about your visitor? Would you ask Jesus to help you to do your work as efficiently as possible? How would your work change? Are there things you do at your job that you would change because Jesus were by your side?

Lunch time would come, and Jesus would be there to share your meal. Would you allow Him to raise His hands in blessing over your lunch? Would you bow your head and return thanks just to show Him that you do that? Perhaps you share your meal with some of your associates at work. If you do and you knew Jesus was by your side, would your conversation with your work associates change? Would you eat the same food? Then after the meal, it would be back to work. Jesus would be there with you every minute.

What would you talk about with Him? It would not be polite to not even recognize His presence near you, would it? Would you be embarrassed at His presence and just avoid Him?

On the way home from work, would you take Him shopping with you? If you did, He would save you a lot of money on your grocery bill. He would suggest ways to be more efficient. He would help you organize your time. He would remind you of things you needed that would save you a trip to town later. He knows your needs for today as well as for next week. After shopping you would return home. How would your television viewing change? Would you invite Him to watch the 6:00 news with you? Do you have some evening programs that you would forgo seeing since Jesus was with you? If you have a spouse or family at your home, how would your relationship change if you knew Jesus was by your side? Would you invite your family to enter the conversation you were having with Him? Would the menu change a little? As the evening progressed, it would be impolite to avoid your heavenly guest wouldn't it? You would need to do something. How would your week change? Jesus mentioned that He was coming for a week. Would you gather your family around Him for worship on the evening of His first day with you?

There would be a day of worship during the week that He came to visit with you. How would your day of worship change? Would it be the same? How would you feel at church if all the members there knew that Jesus was visiting with you for the week? Would your discussion with them change? How would you spend the afternoon on that day of worship? Wouldn't it be nice if you asked Jesus to plan your afternoon activities? There is a concept I have been trying to follow for several weeks now. It is tithing my time every hour. With this practice, I consciously turn my thoughts to Jesus a minimum of 6 minutes out of every hour. This one concept is changing my life. The goal of course is to maintain continual communion with Jesus, but 6 minutes out of every hour is more than I have done in the past. I urge you to make a conscious effort to turn to Christ and pray to Him or make yourself aware of His presence at least 6 minutes out of every hour. Then try to increase the time until you have formed a habit of turning to Him moment by moment.

I was reading a book called Christ Object Lessons. On page 421, a statement came to my attention. "To His faithful followers, Christ has been a daily companion and familiar friend. They have lived in close contact, in constant communion with God. Upon them, the glory of the Lord has risen. In them, the light of the knowledge of the glory of God, in the face of Jesus Christ has been reflected. Now they rejoice in the undimmed rays of the brightness and glory of the King in His majesty. They are prepared for the communion of heaven; for they have heaven in their hearts." COL 421. There are a people who know Jesus. Are you one of them? Here is another statement from the same inspirational writer. "All who follow the Lamb in heaven will first have followed Him on earth, in trustful, loving, willing obedience, followed Him not fretfully and capriciously, but confidently, truthfully, as the flock follows the shepherd." 3 Selected Messages 424

Make the rest of this week the week that Jesus comes to visit you. You may enjoy it so much, finding such satisfaction in His presence, that you will desire to make this entire year the year Jesus came to your home.

"If any man will come after me, let him deny himself, and take up his cross, and follow me."
Matthew 16:24

Day Ten

It is another one of those beautiful spring days. Shortly after I awoke, my thoughts turned to Jesus. I did not write in this journal in the evening as I usually do. It is the morning of the next day. I continued to consciously contact Jesus for those 6 minutes out of every hour. Some hours were more, a few were less but even this little amount of time with Him is special. There were some things He brought to my attention. I recently heard that the average American lies at least once every 10 minutes. So, we discussed ways to keep my communication with others honest. On more than one occasion yesterday, as I played back to Jesus what I had said, I found that I had exaggerated things. This is a form of lying. I ask Him to flag any untruthful speech and He did. After a short time, I took a little more time to answer, to check what I was about to say with the measuring rod of truth. One of the first text I mentioned to you in this journal came again to mind. *"My dear brothers and sisters be quick to listen, slow to speak, and slow to get angry.* Psalm 95:6-7 (NLT). I am becoming a little slower to speak now. It is important to Jesus that those who claim His name show fruits in their lives that are representative of Christ.

There were a few other texts He recalled along these lines. Of the special group who are to follow the Lamb wherever He goes, one of the characteristics they have developed in their lives is truthfulness. *"No lie was found in their mouths; they are blameless."* Revelation 14:5, (NIV). God does not lie. Some Bible translations state that He cannot lie. *"A faith and knowledge resting on the hope of eternal life, which God, who does not lie, promised before the beginning of time."* Titus 1:2, (NIV). Jesus said of Himself in John 14:6, (KJV). *"I am the way, the truth, and the life: no man cometh unto the Father, but by me."* Also, those who are in Christ will have the indwelling presence of the Holy Spirit. Truthfulness is also a trait given to Him. *"When the Counselor comes, whom I will send to you from the Father, the Spirit of truth, he will testify of me."* John 15:26, (KJV).

As these texts and thoughts went through my mind, I tried to carry truthfulness to its complete fulfillment in one's life. From a child, the phrase "It is better to die than tell a lie," has been instilled within. But to carry truthfulness to its complete fulfilment will require the continual help of Jesus. It is topics like this that we can discuss with Jesus. In your communion with Him today, you could ask Him; "What is a lie, Jesus?" Then listen for His response. As you discuss truthfulness with Him, He could let you know how you are measuring up to this standard. If the average person lies several times a day in either word or action, then there is a good possibility that we are not being completely truthful in our interactions with those around us. "No man is an island." Weaknesses of one will more than likely show up in the rest of us, at least occasionally.

My business participated in a home and garden show to educate the community about our landscape services. At first, the response rate was extremely low. After several hours, we only had 5 leads. I talked to Jesus about it. One of the traits of the serving Christian is giving. We are told to *"Remember the words of the Lord Jesus, how he said, it is more blessed to give than to receive."* Acts 20:35. With this reminder He gave me, I started asking people if they would like to enter a drawing for $1,000.00 toward their landscape needs. There were over a hundred lead cards in a small box. By the time the show was finished, we had 89 of them filled out. People started to open and discuss their needs with us. Several potentials, good quality job opportunities came out of this. Again, the *"Quick to listen,"* portion of the above text came to mind. I was giving God the glory in my mind for the sudden turn of interest when what appeared to be a prominent family stopped by. I could tell they were no strangers to wealth. They had 4 children with them. All of them had stylish clothes. Their hair had been professionally done. I was impressed. When I offered the lady a card and asked if she would like to enter the drawing, she did not accept it. She and her husband went closer to the display and seemed to be checking every little detail out. I let them look and talked a few minutes with a couple of other families that stopped by, then turned my attention back to them. What followed was quite amazing.

They are associated with an information, activities center in the area. This center hosts up to 79,000 visitors a year. Families that come to see if they would like to move into the area stop there to pick up local information. They sponsor tours and community programs that bring residents from the area to their facility. This family had viewed the other landscapers displays at the show and decided that our company would best fit their needs. We have been asked to put up a permanent display there with waterfalls, landscaping, etc. We will have a permanent sign and they will pass out our cards or brochures to any inquiring individuals. It is a great opportunity to show those who plan to settle in the area what our landscape service can provide them with.

Three other families or individuals stopped by who have large, 3-4-acre parcels of land they would like landscaped. One of them was a $1,000.00 winner. Another family are putting in an amusement park and wants us to set down with them and design some landscape plans for their project. This project could turn out to be very profitable. They want waterfalls, brooks, patios, plantings, and ponds interspersed throughout the whole area. A Physician wants us to design and price out an indoor waterfall for him. These were a few of the many interest generated after talking to Jesus about it. What if I had not invited Him to show me how to improve the effectiveness of our advertising? There would have been a lot fewer response. We would have gone home from the show wondering why we even bothered. It is great to have a friend who is interested in us so intimately that He will share ways to live life more fully, and truthfully while demonstrating how we can serve our fellow humans more effectively. If we consistently devote time to Him, invite Him to be our counselor in every aspect of our lives, and seek to meet the needs of others, He will more than meet any needs we may have.

Ephesians 3:20-21

"Now to him who can do immeasurable more than all we ask or imagine, according to his power that is at work within us, to him be glory in the church and in Christ Jesus throughout all generations, for ever and ever! Amen.

Day Eleven

How are things going? By now if you have been reading one day at a time and following some of the material, you will have heard the guiding voice of Jesus speaking to you. Some of you could even now be living so close to Jesus, He has sent you to do specific things for Him. Others may still be struggling with finding His voice or making the time to listen to it. Most of us have heard Him speaking to us but do not continue to listen all day long. Our enemy will try to fill up our time. He will try to drown out the voice of Jesus with the noises surrounding us. The blaring radio in the background or the television keep the subconscious mind so busy filtering through all that stuff, it has less time to put us into contact with our Creator. Do not get discouraged if you do not feel you have reached the results you desire. We get in a habit of doing things a certain way and it will take the formation of new habits to overcome the old ones. Keep reaching out to Jesus and you will find He has been reaching out to you.

I had a remarkably busy day. I made out a schedule and ask Jesus to help me fit it all in. We got through it all except one detail. I had to cancel one appointment because we had a batch of cement coming in for the project we were working on. Cement needs the attention of someone who knows what must be done in the short time we have to work with it. It all worked out. There were times though, when things popped out of nowhere and cried for attention. It is easy at these times, to forget to keep up the friendship with our unseen companion. He was with me today though. He even scheduled the cement for me because I probably would not have gotten to it in the time frame needed. How did Jesus manage to do this? Another contractor was working on a different project on the same grounds. He needed about a yard and a half of cement. It is more costly for a cement truck to deliver small batches like that, so the contractor asks how much cement I needed. I had just taken the measurements and was figuring it out.

"We'll schedule your cement with ours," he told me. He asks how much I needed and said he would order that much extra. I figured we needed close to 10 yards. Working through this contractor though, the amount I thought I needed was a yard too much. So, Jesus worked it out for both of us. Eight yards came in first and I was expecting another 3 ½ yards, but the other contractor did not order the extra until he knew how far the first load went. Then estimating the amount of area left, they only ordered that much. It saved us around a hundred dollars. While I was going to appointments, Jesus would suggest other things I could do while in the different areas that would save time later. When I did talk to Jesus, He shared some things with me about trust.

Jesus is looking for a group of people in these closing days of earth's history that He can trust completely. The people He wants will have come to the place in their spiritual experience where they can be trusted to do whatever He tells them to do and say whatever He tells them to say. Though, everyone who is expecting to enter in through the gates of the New Jerusalem will have to be trustworthy. Jesus must be able to trust them with eternity. *"End all wickedness, O Lord, and bless all who truly worship God, for you, the righteous God, look deep within the hearts of men and women and examine all their motives and their thoughts."* Psalm 7:9, (NIV). If we do not prove we will obey Him during His examination with us, He will not be able to use us. If we cannot be used of Christ for the purpose, He has for us here, we will not prove to Him that we are willing to go where He wants us to go, do what He wants us to do, be what He wants us to be and say what He wants us to say. It would not be safe for Him to take us to heaven, so He will not. Sin will not raise a second time. Once this life is over and the earth created anew, the sin chapter of the universe will be written, finished, completed never to appear again throughout eternity. Do you feel Jesus could trust you to do what He ask you to do? Do you feel you could do it for the rest of eternity? Can you be trusted with eternal life?

There are specific things Jesus wants us to do for Him. There are specific people He wants us to reach for Him. He has some very personal information He wants us to share with others. We are to share the Gospel of truth with them. We need to be so used to doing His will without questioning Him, that when we are told to go somewhere, we go, when we are asked to do something for Him, we do it, when He gives us a message to share, we share it just the way He ask us to. *"For we speak as messengers from God, trusted by him to tell the truth. We don't speak to please men, but to please God who test our hearts."* 1 Thessalonians 2:4, (NLT). Jesus sent each of His disciples on specific mission trips. They raised up churches all over the world. His commands were their marching orders. There is a time soon when the Holy Spirit will be poured out with great power. Christ will again have disciples all over the world following His commands. This time they will be under the guiding Spirit of Christ. All of them will be instructed at the same time to help Him in the completion of the gospel work on earth. If we are not being led by the Spirt of Christ now in our everyday activities, do we expect that He will suddenly entrust us with a great measure of His Power? Are we mistaken in believing that one day we will be going about life in our own, usual way–with hardly a thought of Him or His work on earth–and the next day suddenly transformed into an effective army for Christ, to move at the Holy Spirits command? If we have this idea, then we have a mistaken idea of how things will end.

He is measuring us now. Today, this very day is to be the training time. Today we must listen for His voice and follow the missions He wants to send us on. If you hear His voice speaking to you now, follow it. Do what He commands you to do. The more you follow His commands, the greater will be the work you are entrusted with. If you follow little you will receive little or nothing and what little you have will be taken away and given to someone who will obey.

There is a parable that comes to mind as I close this session with you. This parable is for me as well as for any reader of this material. We can enter it and ask our self a particularly important question. Can Jesus trust us with even a little? Because of space, we will enter the parable halfway though.

"*The man with the two talents also came. 'Master he said, 'you entrusted me with two talents; see, I have gained two more.' His master replied, 'Well done, good and faithful servant! You have been faithful with a few things; I will put you in charge of many things. Come and share your master's happiness! Then the man who had received the one talent came. 'Master,' he said, 'I knew that you are a hard man, harvesting where you have not sown and gathering where you have not scattered seed. So, I was afraid and went out and hid your talent in the ground. See, here is what belongs to you.' His master replied, 'You wicked, lazy servant! So, you knew that I harvested where I have not sown and gather where I have not scattered seed?*

Well then, you should have put my money on deposit with the bankers so that when I returned, I would have received it back with interest. Take the talent from him and give it to the one who has the ten talents. For everyone who has will be given more, and he will have an abundance. Whoever does not have, even what he has will be taken from him. Now throw this worthless servant outside, into the darkness, where there will be weeping and gnashing of teeth.'" Matthew 25:22-30, (NLT).

Psalm 139:23-24

"Search me, O God, and know my heart; test me and know my thoughts. Point out anything in me that offends you and lead me along the path of everlasting life."

Day Twelve

Several minutes this morning before the sun was to makes its appearance from behind the mountain to our east, the Lord woke me. I spent some time in praise to Him. We discussed areas of my life that needed to be surrendered to Him. I was about to close the session when He reminded me to study His Word. I rose and went into the office to get my colored pens and Bibles. I selected three of them. One Bible has four parallel versions. There is the King James, the New International Version, The Living Bible and The Revised Standard Version. The story about how this came into my possession may be of interest to you. Sometime I would like to sit down with several inspirational writers and question them about how they are informed on what to write in their books.

For me, certain themes come into my mind. Yesterday, for instance the theme was on trust. Can Jesus trust us with eternal life? The day before was on being truthful in all that we do and speak. As I communicated with my Lord this morning, I ask Him what theme I should write about. The word death came to mind. I questioned His leading. If we have The Author of Life by our side, why would we want to think about death? We have so little time to live. Our life is but a breath compared to eternity. Perhaps the subject of death is something that is on your mind lately. Perhaps there are some issues dealing with it you need resolved. If so, perhaps this day will help. As of now I have no idea what these fingers will produce on the computer. So, the adventure begins.

I wish the individual who gave me that Bible had signed it. I cannot even remember his name. Perhaps it will come to me before the end of this journal entry. Our church had recently completed a training session with Elder Don Gray on how to study the Bible with others. A mailing had gone out in our community and around 75 responses came back. Our pastor went on the first study or two with each of the members who had volunteered to give Bible studies then we were on our own with our Lord and those who were interested in learning more about Him. This man was one of two studies I was giving. Most of the time his son would come to the study. I learned later, after his death, that he considered me his pastor. His son called our home to ask me to conduct his father's funeral, but we were out of state visiting relatives at the time. It was not until several weeks later I learned he had died. After studying with him for over a year, he was no closer to embracing the truths we had gone over than the first week, so my pastor suggested I should not study with him and move on. We finished the Don Gray studies and went through The Encounter Series. At every study he would have his mug of alcohol in front of him.

He seldom filled in the blanks, so we did it at the meeting. The first Christmas he presented me with this Parallel Bible. I gave him a book. I believe it was Bible Readings for the Home. His son informed me that he died believing in Jesus and one of his last requests was for me to come and see him, but I was out of state.

This morning, as I read from the gospel of John the account of Jesus walking with Peter along the shore was the subject. Jesus asked Peter if he loved Him, not once, not twice, but three times. "Simon, son of John, do you love me more than these?" John 21:15, (NIV). After asking Peter three times if he loved Him, Jesus informed him of how he would die. Why would Jesus tell a person how they were to die? What purpose could He have in doing that? Let us continue the story so you can understand what we are talking about. I will use the Revised Standard Version portion of the Parallel Bible I received from my alcoholic friend. "Truly, truly, I say to you, when you were young, you girded yourself and walked where you would; but when you are old, you will stretch out your hands, and another will gird you and carry you where you do not wish to go." (This he said to show by what death he was to glorify God.) And after this he said to him, 'Follow me.'" John 21:18-19, (NIV).

Several years ago, I absented myself from church one day to spend the time in fasting and prayer. I drove to a place overlooking Lake Michigan and with Bibles and study material, I prepared for a time of wonderful communion with Jesus. He came remarkably close to me that day. Our conversation was on a friend-to-friend basis. During our time together by the lake, Jesus laid out His plans for me. By the time the day was finished, I was thoroughly committed to doing all that He planned. Unfortunately, I did not follow in the path He had chosen for me so plan two or three came to be. He did share with me what death I would experience though if I followed the path He had marked out. This was not a pleasant revelation. I had always planned to be as John puts it later in the chapter, "If it is my will that he remains until I come, what is that to you?" John 21:23, (RSV).

What thoughts enter your mind when you think about your own death? Are you afraid to close your life here on earth? If so, what is the source of your fear? For me it is the association of pain with death. Nearly everyone who has died so far during the existence of sin has suffered some degree of pain at death. So far, I have led a relatively pain free life. I would like to keep it that way. Would I give up eternal life to avoid pain? Jesus suffered the greatest pain of all before His death. He was tortured beyond human endurance. His blood was shed on the dusty streets from the judgment hall to the place of the skull. He had pain with each drop that fell to the ground but the greatest pain He had to endure was the pain of separation from His Father when the crushing weight of my sin and yours came down upon Him. As I was considering the pain I will most likely suffer before death, Jesus reminded me of the pain He will suffer if He goes throughout eternity without me. "Yet what we suffer now is nothing compared to the glory he will give us later. For all creation is waiting patiently and hopefully for the future day when God will resurrect his children. For on that day thorns and thistles, sin, death, and decay–the things that overcame the world against its will at God's command–will all disappear, and the world around us will share in the glorious freedom from sin which God's children enjoy." Romans 8:18-21, (NIV).

It is one thing to die with the hope of eternal life and another to die and be lost, forever separated from the one who loved us so much, He saw us fit to bring into existence so He could share eternity with us. Consider the loss you would feel if you knew a son or daughter, a spouse or parent would not walk those golden streets with you in glory because they chose to separate themselves from their Creator here on earth. I am crying out to you Dear Reader. If you are living your life without Jesus now, if you choose to not make Him a presence in your daily life, turn, turn to Him now and ask Him to change your priorities. Do this if you really love Him. Do it if you really crave a living friendship with Jesus. Are you putting afar off the time when you will yield completely to Him? Do not delay a moment longer. "*Behold, now is the acceptable time; behold, now is the day of salvation.*" 2 Corinthians 6:2, (NIV). The Author of life is standing by. He has made Himself available to you. If you choose to follow Him, not even death will be able to separate you from Him.

It was the last load of personal items to be moved from Michigan to Washington. I was driving a 4x4 Ford Ranger towing a 16' car hauler loaded with three tons of prized possessions. I had completed about half of my journey when the trailer started to sway. You must experience this to understand what it feels like to suddenly know everything is out of control. My truck was turned around. The trailer was pulling me with it down a steep hill to certain destruction. On one side of the road, a deep ravine would be my landing place if the guardrail did not hold. On the other side, the meridian tilted at a very steep angle. I only had time for a short prayer before I felt my end might come. It is at times like this–when death is staring you in the face–that your mind focuses on what really matters in life. I wanted to spend eternity with Jesus, so He was first on my mind. I made a quick request that He forgive me of my sins then braced myself for the crash that was sure to come. It hit. The bumping, scraping, skidding being slammed again and again into the guard rail like a cork on a string, then it was over. I could not get out of the door on the driver's side because it was tight against the railing. There was stuff in the passenger's seat, but I managed to crawl over it and open that door to check the damage. The truck was not bad. The trailer had one flat tire. It could be fixed. Some of my things were scattered on the canyon floor far below, one of them–possibly the tire arm I needed to change the tire. I was surveying the damage when my brother-in-law and his family came by going the other direction. I was heading from Michigan to Washington. They were heading from Oregon to Minnesota. It was a chance in a million encounter, but it came, and he had what I needed to change the tire and be on the move again. Throughout that journey, I was convinced of Jesus' protection over me again and again. He was sparing my life for some purpose. Death currently was not in His plan.

As I looked at all the stuff I was carrying, it was nothing compared to eternal life. Jesus was trying to tell me not to get wrapped up in physical possessions. *"Donielle, son of William, do you love me more than these?"* I was a slow learner though. Twice more the trailer took my truck where it would on that most memorial road trip of my life. Twice more portions of my possessions were scattered along the highway. Twice more death stared me in the face and my soul was laid bare before the judgment bar of God. It was my Peter experience with Jesus.

The second time it happened I found myself in a deep ditch. The highway was covered in ice. There was a coat of sleet over everything. In this ditch, every blade of grass was fat with icy crystals. I looked around and picked up a few things that were scattered around. Then with a prayer on my lips, I placed the truck in low 4x4 and started driving against the traffic while still in the ditch. When I could see nothing coming, I drove up the steep bank pulling that trailer. A county truck had just passed and stopped. To this day I believe the angels of heaven were pushing or pulling me up that bank. The truck made it all the way to the top. I did a U-turn onto the icy covered freeway to go the same way as the traffic. As I passed the county truck, the two men in the cab were shaking their heads with unbelief. I quickly got into the slow lane because there, barreling down upon me, was a semi-truck. I shudder to think of what would have happened had I been spinning or stuck across that icy freeway. There is no way the driver could have stopped.

By the third time the trailer swayed out of control and turned around, I was in total submission to my Lord and Savior. It happened in the days before cell phones were so common. I could not just stand up and call for help. On the third time, believe-it-or-not, a different brother-in-law came to my rescue. What are the odds of that happening? I only have 4 brothers-in-law and they were scattered over 3 states. By that time, the trailer was a total wreck, but the truck was miraculously intact. The trailer would have survived had a drunk driver not tried to pass me on the wrong side. He rode up over the back of the trailer, went into the ditch and out again. He stopped only long enough to see if I was OK then because of his drinking, sped off scattering broken parts of his van along the road as he went.

Sometimes, Jesus must talk to us real loudly to get our attention. He gives us warning after warning. His grace does have a limit though. Has He warned you lately? Perhaps He has called out to you not once or twice but three times or more. If He has, do not delay in answering Him. Avail yourself of the life He is offering to you now. Death could knock on your door at any moment. *"Behold, now is the acceptable time; behold, now is the day of salvation."* 2 Corinthians 6:2.

Psalm 23:4

"Even when walking through the dark valley of death I will not be afraid, for you are close beside me, guarding, guiding all the way."

Day Thirteen

How is your week going so far? If you submitted your life to His care and keeping this morning when He woke you, your day has been or will be better because of Him. Have you recently felt a sense of His presence near you? Have you sensed His deep love for you? How is your relationship with your family going? If Jesus is becoming a constant companion at your side, then others should *"take note of you that you have been with Jesus."* The call to Christianity is the call to service. We are to serve our fellow human brothers and sisters. In my work, I do not always keep this in mind. I still have a lot in me that wants to crop up and take control. It is a struggle to think of others. A few moments ago, I went to get a bottle of juice. I was halfway up the stairs when Jesus mentioned to bring one up to my wife. I did and she appreciated it. At times He suggest that I make breakfast for her or the evening meal. She is very appreciative of this. When I meddle in the little chores around the house to help keep things in order, she notices and thanks me. When our love for Jesus is in order, He increases our love for those around us and especially those closest to us. We are in the world for one purpose. It is not to serve ourselves. It is not to see how much money we can accumulate. It is not to make this world our home. It is to share the love of the Savior with those who need His salvation. That includes all of us. We are all part of the family of God albeit there are a lot of our brothers and sisters who are lost. For them, this world is their home. It is all they know and all they believe they will have. They do not share the hope of eternal life we have. How can we bring the Jesus we are becoming ever increasingly close to, into their lives so He can work His will in them?

I was traveling by train back from my mother's funeral. My wife and son had left a week earlier. I stayed by to be with Dad and it was good I did for he followed her in death a few months later. There is something about losing a mother or father that causes a person to think about the future, not the earthly future but the heavenly one. I was in close contact with Jesus during this ride and ask if it was His will, to bring me someone to talk to. I wanted a special person, one who was remarkably close to Jesus. I was hurting inside and needed a sympathizing ear. I needed someone who had faced what I was going through. I needed some heavenly encouragement. I sent this request to the companion by my side and hoped He would answer. The answer did not take long to come. Not more than five minutes later, a middle-aged woman came through the door and sat down with a young woman in the seat behind me. I usually do not try to listen into people's conversations but hers was so unusual, my ears became wide open. I found out later the young woman was the niece of the lady and she had spent a portion of the night talking with her Lord about how to reach her for Jesus. The young woman had a Christian background but had wandered away from her belief in spiritual things. The lady's testimony was enormously powerful. At the age of 11, her Baptist father had acquired a book from a colporteur. As he read from its pages, he found the author shared beliefs on what he termed as legalistic. To him the book was poison. He placed it on top of the bookcase and when he saw his daughter eyeing it one day, forbid her to read it. Being a curious girl however, she would take it down and read it while he was at work, always careful to place it back exactly how he had left it. In time she accepted the message of the book. She lived by the ocean and would often take the book to her favorite rock overlooking the bay. There she would talk to her Jesus. One day as she was talking with Him, He spoke clearly to her mind. His words thrilled her and changed her life forever.

"But now Betty, the Lord who created you says; "do not be afraid, for I have redeemed you. I have called you by name; you are mine. When you go through the deep waters, I will be with you. When the rivers of difficulty rise, you will not drown! When you walk through the fire, you will not be burned, the flames will not consume you. For I am the Lord, your God, the Holy one, your Savior." Isaiah 43:1-3. After that assurance from Jesus, she turned her life over to Him completely and as the years progressed, grew ever closer to her beloved.

The Lord had shared with her during her night session with Him how to reach her niece. As the girl listened to her aunt, tears began to come to her eyes and when the time was right, Betty led her to the throne of grace right there on the train with all those people around. The lesson was one of sublime importance to me. When the time is right, people need to be given the opportunity to accept the salvation Jesus offers. After the prayer, the girl rose and went into another car while the lady remained to thank Jesus. I leaned back to her and remarked about her testimony. She had another mission Jesus had impressed on her but promised to return and talk to me in a couple of hours. She did and my heart thrilled to see how close Jesus wishes to come to us. He wants to inhabit our existence. He wants to settle down in our heart and make it His permanent home.

I received the comfort I needed. When I was hurting, He provided an ear to listen. She had recently been through what I had, only it was the loss of her father, not her mother. She was thrilled to tell me that on his deathbed, he had accepted the truths he had tried to shelter her from. The Lord had used her to bring to her father a greater knowledge of God. I shared with her the experience my mother had with Jesus a week before her death and Betty again shared how the Lord had in the past and continued to communicate with her in a personal way. She was there on that train by Divine appointment, partly for her niece, partly for me to build up my faith in Jesus and partly for any other appointments

Jesus needed her for. Her life was not an easy one. Her husband did not understand her drive to be all Jesus wanted her to be. He was jealous of the time she spent with others. I encouraged her to keep up the good work, to follow her heart and Jesus would work out things with her husband. In a letter from her, she mentioned that was happening. Upon leaving, Betty thanked me for the encouragement I had brought to her also.

There are people all around us who are hurting. Satan has bound them in chains of vice. They struggle in vain to escape from his clutches. The only way out for them is through Jesus. They need to talk with someone who knows the way of Salvation. They need to see Christ working in the life of a fellow human. They need to hear my testimony and yours. When we have Jesus beside us, He will if we are willing, fill up our day with appointments for the Kingdom of Heaven. As we reach out to those struggling ones beside us, Jesus reaches out through us and draws them to Him. *"Then Jesus told them, 'The voice was for your benefit, not mine. The time of judgment for the world has come when the prince of this world will be cast out. And when I am lifted on the cross, I will draw everyone to myself."* John 12:30-32, (NLT). Satan's claim over people can and will be broken as those who are in Christ Jesus become instruments of His grace. Jesus was lifted on the cross and those who are lost are being drawn to Him. We are given the privilege of pointing them to their up-lifted Savior. It is a sacred responsibility. Once they are shown the way of Salvation, they need an ally who can check up on them occasionally to bring continued encouragement in the way. We need to encourage our fellow brothers and sisters in Jesus also. Yesterday in our discussion about Peter, after He acknowledged his love for Jesus, Jesus requested that he feed His lambs, His sheep, and His little sheep. After Jesus pointed out the way, He was to glorify God through death, He said to Peter, "Follow me."

If we are following Jesus, He will lead us in a Christian walk that is ever growing. It will be a vibrant, exciting life. He will wake us up each morning and tell us what He wants us to do. Our Christian way of life will not stagnate because we will not only see Jesus leading in our own life, but we will also see Him at work in the lives of others. When He sends us on Divine appointments, we will thrill at how He has arranged circumstances to bring others into contact with us. We can talk to Him beside us now and ask Him to have His way in our life. As we follow His prompting, there will be encouragement in our Christian walk. All of us need a little Divine Assurance from time to time. We all need to feel the power of God at work in our lives. Ask and you will receive. This is how we are to grow up in Christ Jesus, grow every day closer and closer to Him until we enter in through those pearly gates of the New Jerusalem, there to ever be with our Lord and those who are there because of the appointments Jesus has sent us on.

While reviewing this book before publishing, I received a text message on my phone. It was my daughter-in-law. My son recently re-committed his life to Jesus. He is on fire for the Lord. But sometimes his enthusiasm gets out of bounds. He was sharing some scary passages with his wife from the Bible. Her faith is growing but she is still a tender plant that needs nourishment and milk of the Word. The scary passages got her worked up to the point where she could not sleep and was imagining thing that might never happen. She appealed to me as to what to do. As I looked back over what I had reviewed, the day I spoke about angels came to mind, so I texted her back to remember the guarding angel by her side. Neither the devil nor evil men can get past that angel if one places their trust in Jesus. She texted back about her greatest fear. She stated if this came to pass, she would not be able to endure it. Jesus reminded me of a passage in the Bible. I will paraphrase it. *The Lord will not allow us to be tempted beyond what we are able to handle but will with the temptation provide a way of escape.* Then I assured her Jesus could be trusted. That He cannot lie and will do exactly what He says He will do. She thanked me and said it was just what she needed. Now she could sleep and get the rest she needed for growing within her is a little one who by the time this book is published will have made her entrance into this world. *If God cares for the little sparrows will He not care for you? are you not of more value than them?* Was it a divine appointment? I believe it was.

Will there be another divine appointment, soon? I do not know. This is part of moment-by-moment experiences we will have when we allow Jesus to direct our life. A couple of days ago while talking with Jesus, I felt impressed to visit our pastor. He was helping one of his churches in a remodeling project and fell off a ladder. So that day I made the trip to the hospital. He was in bad shape. His face had several bruises on it from the fall. He had 4 fractured ribs, a punctured lung, broken arm, and fractured pelvis. I do not know how in the coming weeks he will be able to do anything without a lot of pain. I went there in hopes of encouraging him, but things got turned around. He was smiling. He was pleasant and upbeat. His spirits were particularly good. "*Unbelievable*," I thought to myself. He should be using this time for self-pity. In the end perhaps that divine appointment was meant to increase my spiritual growth rather than give him encouragement. I may never know.

Isaiah 40:4-5

"The Lord God has given me the tongue of the learned, that I should know how to speak a word in season to him who is weary. He awakens me morning by morning; He awakens my ear to hear as the learned. The Lord God has opened my ear; and I was not rebellious, nor did I turn away from hearing Him."

Day Fourteen

Greetings! How did your day with Jesus go? Did He send you on any Divine appointments? I have my laptop computer near my bed. I will start it up often before I get up. While writing this journal, I keep playing the messages over and over in my mind. If the message is good, it is better for me because I am well acquainted with what I have written by the time it is revised two or three times. During the night, mistakes come to mind, or ways to state a concept more clearly, so in the morning I often make those corrections. That is what happened this morning, I thought of a better way to present something I wrote yesterday so turned on the computer without the power source plugged in. With a laptop computer it is good to run the battery all the way down every now and then. So, by the time the changes were made, I got out of bed, about half of the power was used up. We traveled with some friends to a resort. We were to be there for a few days. It was about a four-hour trip. After checking in and having a bite to eat, I was anxious to get to this entry. I retired to our suite while the others were watching videos. My time with Jesus has become more important to me than spending time with a video for an hour and a half or more. I was ready to start my writing, but Jesus had other plans. He set up a Divine appointment for me. My friend asked me to go for a walk along the beach. I did not want to go. I wanted to write and was about to pass up the walk when this laptop froze up. Somehow the manufacturers did not put a disconnect switch on it like I have seen on other models. So, the only way to shut it off is to let the battery run down completely, then the computer goes into hibernation. There was another way. I could unscrew the battery compartment and disconnect it but why? Jesus had other plans for me. I got the hint. I could not write for at least half an hour, so I went on the walk. Jesus wanted me to go on that walk and share with my friend some of the great times I was having with Him as my friend and companion. He was still hurting from the death of his father. The entry I wrote a couple of days ago on death was a help. I was able to bring some of that to him as we talked. Now I know why Jesus wanted me to explore the topic of death. He knew of this friend's need two days before I did. By the time I got back from the walk, the computer was hibernating and with one punch of the button, I was able to continue writing. I also had the room to myself so I could be more attentive to the guiding voice of Jesus.

When I get wrapped up in duties that come with friendship, I miss the time I have Jesus to myself. I am trying to learn how to take Him with me. It is kind of selfish for me to want time with Him alone. He has so much He wants to share with others. I sometimes forget that I am not the only person He loves. His love to every fellow human is everlasting. He wants all of them to accept the gift of eternal life. He won for us when He cried "It is finished." My friend was also having some problems with a teenage son. There seemed to be a lack of respect. The dad felt he should receive just because he was the father. His son and mine are close friends. One day while driving with them, my friend's son said some positive things about his father. As we walked and talked, I shared with the father those good qualities his son admired him for, and it brought a lot of relief to the father. I will write his statement here for your encouragement if you are having trouble with someone close to you. The father, after hearing the good things his son had said about him made this statement.

"Well, it looks like I am not a complete failure as a father, because there are some things my son admires me for." That made the walk worthwhile. I could rejoice knowing the father could still have hope that the problems he was having could possibly be resolved sometime. Before the walk, I was going to write on another topic. The one that came to mind as I talked with Jesus on the way to the resort was covetousness and contentment. I will move in that direction now. We are told in Hebrews 13:5, (KJV). "*Let your conversation be without covetousness; and be content with such things as ye have: for he hath said, I will never leave thee, nor forsake thee.*"

What about contentment? Are you content? Are there things you covet? We are told that Covetousness is the sin of this age. As I look at the members of my church family, I wonder how deep does covetous run. The church was brought into existence to serve the world. She was to be an agent of The Father's Salvation through Jesus Christ. She was not to make her home here. Her place was with her betrothed, Jesus in the most beautiful home ever created for a bride. Jesus spared nothing in making it the best it could possibly be. As he watched His beloved, He could hardly wait for the day when He would be united with her. But His beloved sought out a thousand other lovers. She lowered her standards to the darkest depths. Still, He loved her, still He went after her time and time again, trying to woo her back into His arms. She was not content with what He promised her though. Covetousness caused her to eventually divorce herself from Him.

"It has been said, 'If a man divorces his wife, and she go away from him to become another man's, shall her first husband return to her again? Shall not that land be greatly polluted?' But you have played the harlot with many lovers; yet return to me, says the LORD. Lift your eyes to the high places and see where you have not been laid with. You sat waiting for them by the wayside, as the Arabian in the wilderness; you polluted the land with your adultery and with your wickedness. Therefore, the

showers have been taken from you, and there has not been any latter rain. Adulteress was written on your forehead, but you refused to be ashamed. Will the time ever come when you cry unto me, my father, you are the guide of my youth? Will you reserve your anger forever? Will you keep it to the end? Behold, you have spoken and done evil things. The LORD also said to me in the days of Josiah the king, 'Have you seen all the backsliding Israel has done? She is gone up upon every high mountain and under every green tree, and there hath played the harlot. And I said after she had done all these things, Turn, turn back to me. But she did not return." Jeremiah 3:1-7 (NKJV).

What can the world give us? What future do we have here? It is coming to an end. Why invest in it a moment longer? It is a sinking ship, a doomed lifestyle. Why, O why do we seek friendship with everyone but Jesus? When it is convenient, we appear in public with Him on our arm but when the darkness comes, when no one is looking, we play the harlot. We often do not even wait for the night to come to sin against Him. We depart from Him in front of everyone and are not ashamed of it. The mark of our sin is clearly visible to all. We, at times, appear proud of our rebellion against Him. We covet and go after the pleasures of sin while Jesus waits in the shadows, hoping for the day when we will come back to Him, but we do not return, so the latter rain has not come. Will a man go back to his first wife after she has scorned him, time and time again? Some will but most will not. Will Jesus come back to us again if we ask Him? Yes. It is His greatest desire to be with us, in us, by us, guiding us moment by moment, loving us, living out His Divine life within us. *"Live your life without covetousness; and be content with what you have: for he has said, I will never leave you, nor forsake you."* He has not left us; He has not divorced us. He promises to never leave or forsake us. He promises to supply all our needs. When we have Jesus, what more do we need? Nothing, nothing at all for when we really have Him, we have everything. We do not need to covet because we are content.

Malachi 3:7

"'Return to Me and I will return to you,' says the Lord."

Day Fifteen

Good Morning! It may not be morning to you but it is to me so I will say it again. Good Morning! I have been wanting to say that to you for several days now. Our time together is half over. Hopefully by now though, your time with Jesus is just beginning. Hopefully by now you are coming to realize the Treasure beside you, the Pearl of Great Price, the Bright and Morning Star. Good Morning to you and Good Morning Jesus! If I have had any part in helping to make your friendship with Jesus just a little deeper, then praise God. I know I have grown in these last two weeks. I would not trade them for anything. It has been a truly inspiring journey so far. I have seen Jesus go to work in my life in ways that I never imagined He would, two weeks ago. Hopefully, you are experiencing this also. Jesus is at work in your life. This I am sure of. If you have not recognized it yet, you will, soon, I hope. As I meditated on what to write today, I closed my eyes and listened to the sound of the seagulls outside our open window. I heard the happy cries of the children as they went about their play. There was the occasional conversation between a husband and his wife, or a lover with His new bride. My wife and I looked at their car last evening, Just Married was written across the back window in waxy, white letters. The strings that once held some empty cans, still dangled from the bumper, it was a green hatchback. Somewhere a new home had been established. As I looked back over the life I had with my wife, I was inspired. I remember the day we established our own home.

Have you had any recent, inspiring experiences? While at the breakfast, a television program played in the background. It was an inspirational story of a football team who were the underdogs, voted least likely to succeed. All odds were against them, but when inspired by their coach, they went on to victory. Later the clan wanted me to watch a video with them. I would rather spend my time at other things in most cases but since we were on vacation I relented. The video was an inspirational story of two uncles who suddenly found themselves in possession of a nephew. In the story, one of the uncles fell in love and that love was the source of his inspiration. For his beloved, he fought hundreds as the story goes. He overcame every obstacle. In the end though she died in childbirth. What inspires you? What drives you to get up in the morning and go out to wherever you go? What is the motivation factor in your life? What do you live for? As I ask myself that question, the answer to what used to motivate me came to mind. I was motivated by recognition. Recognition drove me to create artwork better than anyone in any of my classes. Recognition motivated me to excel in nearly any area of my life I chose. Recognition may be your motivating drive. It could be love, or power. It could be money or your kids. It could be any number of things. As I thought of inspiration, I wondered what inspired Jesus to leave heaven and come down to this most wicked planet of His creation.

What inspired Jesus to give up His power? What inspired Him to give up His throne next to the Father? What inspired Him to leave the position of Michael the Arch Angel to become the Son of Man? What motivated Him to be born as a baby, grow and work in a Carpenter's shop? Why did He choose twelve disciples, spend three and a half years in ministry then allow Himself to be crucified? What motivated Him? You did. It was you who caused Him to leave all that power behind. His love for you sent Him down here to die. Your love for Him is what He craves. Spending time with you for eternity is what He wants. Today He waited for you to awake. He stood there by your bed and watched the last moments of your sleep. When your consciousness came to you, He waited patiently to see if you would recognize His presence. If your first thoughts were of Him, He smiled on you and imparted some of His power to help fight your spiritual battles. If you took Him with you through the day, you were blessed. If you talked with Him off and on, you were privileged to have The Source of all Knowledge to be your Counselor. If you did not recognize Jesus when you awoke, if you did not turn to Him this morning, if you did not take Him with you throughout the day, do you realize what you missed? What do you live for? What inspires you? What motivates you to get up every morning. Will what motivates and inspires you, last? Can you say with Paul? *"For me to live is Christ."* Philippians 1:21, (KJV).

Hebrews 3:15

"Today if you will hear His voice, harden not your heart."

Day Sixteen

Hello! How are you today? Has it been a good one so far? We are starting the second half of our 30-day journey with Jesus. Thus far we have been with Him on the mountain tops, with the sun shining down on our shoulders while the warm winds blow. We may have been with Him in a valley or two of darkness where the cold chill frost us and we clutch our cloak around us to conserve what little heat we have. Perhaps we have walked with Him along the shores of the ocean when the tide is out and a million barnacles cling to a hundred thousand rocks. I talked with Him by the sea yesterday. We looked in a small tide pool and watched the snails creep slowly across the sand leaving a trail the exact width of their shell. There were little sea creatures that seemed to breath out their tongues every second or so. The little pool swarmed with life. Who was He, I wondered, this man who knew all about me? He was my Creator and theirs. We had things in common, the barnacles and me. We had life. It came from Him. He brought both of us into existence. From time to time, I could sense His strong arm around me. His love was evident and even though it was chilly, it was warm in His presence. We later looked out over the bay where the rocks rolled down to meet the waves and twisted pine trees waited silently for the strong winds that would come to bend them. They were not concerned because their roots were anchored securely to the boulders. He created the trees too. He created the wind. He shaped the waves, each one. As I looked out and watched them roll in one after another, I realized that from the beginning of time they had done so. While there by the sea with Him, He brought another song to my memory.

In fancy I stood by the shore one day, Of the beautiful murmuring sea.
I saw the great crowds as they thronged the way, Of the Stranger of Galilee.
I saw how the man who was blind from birth, in a moment was made to see.
The lame was made whole by the matchless skill, Of the Stranger of Galilee.

And I felt I could love Him forever, so gracious and tender was He!
I claimed Him that day as my Savior, This Stranger of Galilee.

His look of compassion, his words of love, they shall never be forgotten.
When sin sick and helpless He saw me there, This Stranger of Galilee.
He showed me His hands and His riven side, And He whispered "It was for thee.
My burden fell off at the pierced feet, Of the Stranger of Galilee.

I heard Him speak peace to the angry waves,
of that turbulent, raging sea.
And low! At His word are the waters stilled,
This Stranger of Galilee.
A peaceful, a quiet, and holy calm, Now and
ever abides with me.
He holdeth my life in His mighty hands, This
Stranger of Galilee.

Come ye, who are driven, and tempest-tossed,
And His gracious salvation sees.
He'll quiet life's storms with His "Peace, be
still!" This Stranger of Galilee.
He bids me to go and the story tell, What He
ever to you will be.
If only you let Him with you abide, This
Stranger of Galilee.
Oh, my friend, won't you love Him forever?
So gracious and tender is He!
Accept Him today as your Savior, This
Stranger of Galilee.

If you can find the time, take a walk with
Jesus today. Leave your friends and associates
behind. Make it just you and Him. While you
are together, open your heart to Him. Your heart
may be whole, it may be full of love, it may
be overflowing with joy. Perhaps not though.
Perhaps your heart is sad, or lonely, or hurting.
Maybe it is filled with bitterness, or anger. Open
it up to Jesus. If it is whole, He can make it better.
If it is broken, He can mend it. If it is empty, He
can fill it. If it is filled with self, He can replace

it with Himself. We are told that if Christ is on the throne of the heart, self is on the cross. If self is on the throne of the heart though, Christ is on the cross. How is your heart today? The Bible is full of texts about the heart. It is mentioned some 762 times in the King James Version. As I went through some of the 762 verses that mentioned heart, the first one that spoke to me was in the fifth book of the Bible. *"O that there was such a heart in them, that they would fear me, and keep all my commandments always, that it might be well with them, and with their children forever!"* Deuteronomy 5:29, (KJV).

I can hear the loving Stranger of Galilee crying for the people He loved. "O that there was such a heart in them." Wouldn't it be nice to have a heart that kept all the commandments of our loving God and Savior, Jesus Christ? Not only would this heart keep all His commandments, not just for today, not for tomorrow, not for a week, not for 30 days, but always! There is another text in Deuteronomy that speaks of the heart. It is just one chapter over. Jesus quoted it to some of the rulers who were trying to trap Him also. Deuteronomy 6:5, (KJV). *"And thou shalt love the LORD thy God with all thine heart, and with all thy soul, and with all thy might."* It would be nice to love Jesus with all of one's heart, with all of one's soul and with all of ones might. That type of heart would not be divided. There is a text that talks about a divided heart. Here it is. *"Because their heart is divided, they shall be found faulty."*

Hosiah 10:5, (KJV). I do not think we want to have a divided heart, do we? If it is divided, if we seek to serve God one moment and then serve ourselves the next, we have a faulty heart. The only cure for a faulty heart is found in Jesus. Only He can make it whole again.

In Deuteronomy 10:12-13, (KJV), there was another verse that spoke of the heart. Have you ever wondered what Jesus wanted with you? What are the requirements that He has for us? We know that He loves us. We know that He would have left heaven if we were the only one who needed to be given a chance to possess eternal life. But what does He require of us? *"And now, Israel, what doth the LORD thy God require of thee, but to fear the LORD thy God, to walk in all his ways, and to love him, and to serve the LORD thy God with all thy heart and with all thy soul, To keep the commandments of the LORD, and his statutes, which I command thee this day for thy good?"* It is like the earlier text in Deuteronomy, the one where the Lord was hoping for such a people while all the time knowing they would not. Do you love Jesus? Do you love Him with all your heart? Do you love Him with all your mind? Do you love Him with all your soul? Do you love Him with all your might? Is such a heart available to us, a heart that is totally 100% in tune with Jesus? There is one available. Some of us have already had that new heart transplant. Our old heart was so bad He had to remove it and replace it with another. *"A new heart also will I give you, and a new spirit will I put within you: and I will take away the stony heart out of your flesh, and I will give you a heart of flesh."* Ezekiel 36:26. (KJV)

Once we have this new heart it needs to be programmed like a computer. There is a programmer available. I am sure you know who He is. We can be the people He longs for, the ones He cried out for; O *that there was such a heart in them, that they would fear me, and keep all my commandments always, that it might be well with them, and with their children forever!"* Deuteronomy 5:29. How? The programmer will do it all. The Stranger of Galilee, the healer of broken hearts will go to work and "Create a new heart within us," for He will be the one we choose to make a covenant with our heart on that day. *"For this is the covenant that I will make with the house of Israel after those days, saith the Lord; I will put my laws into their mind and write them in their hearts: and I will be to them a God, and they shall be to me a people:"* Hebrews 8:10. (KJV)

If you have not done so already. If you have not taken that walk with Jesus today, do it soon. He need not be a stranger to you. The Stranger of Galilee can become The Immanuel–God with you. When that happens, He will no longer be a stranger but your Beloved. You will know Him, and He will know you. He will be your God and you will be His child. *"He heals the broken hearted and binds up their wounds."* Psalm 119:10 With a heart like that, it will beat for eternity.

Psalm 119:10

"With my whole heart have I sought thee: O let me not wander from thy commandments."

Day Seventeen

Another day has come. As the last few moments of yesterday ticked away, I again turned to my Creator. It is warm inside of Christ. There is shelter there from the winds of life. Christ is the Perfect Dwelling Place. Once under His roof, the soul can rest and be at peace. Do you have trouble sleeping at night? Do horrible dreams come sometimes to haunt you? Are you restless, tossing and turning as your mind plays over the events of the day? If so, before you go to sleep this evening, enter the House of Jesus. He is the perfect house. Perhaps you have never thought of Jesus as a house. He is an open house. The door is always open. He never locks the door to His children though the tormentor of His children is not allowed inside. He and Jesus had a long battle, but Jesus won. In Bible times, there were cities of refuge, places where people could flee and be free. Jesus is a house of refuge. He is a place you can flee to and be free. Let us explore some Bible text that point this out. *"For in Him we live and move and have our being."* Acts 17:28. (KJV) Did you catch that? We live in Him and move around in Him. Here is another one. Moses gave us this assurance in a Psalm 90:1. (NIV) *"Lord, YOU have been our dwelling place for all generations."* The House, Jesus Christ has been around for generations. Many have dwelt in it. But there is still more text that indicate we can dwell in Him. Let us look at another one. Psalm 27:4. (NKJV) *"One thing I have desired of the Lord, that will I seek: That I may dwell in the house of the Lord all the days of my life, to behold the beauty of the Lord, and to inquire in His temple. For in the time of trouble, He shall hide me in His pavilion."* In the House of Jesus, we can behold the beauty of the Lord.

Have you ever considered the Lord beautiful? His ways are beautiful. He creates beautiful things. He prepares beautiful homes for the ones He came to save. He has a beautiful voice. He has a beautiful face. He would like you to come into His house so you can see His face. He told David to seek it. He is telling you and I to seek it. Look at this text and see. *"When you said, 'Seek my face;' my heart said back to you, 'Your face, LORD, will I seek."* Psalm 27:8. (GW)There is double security in the House of Jesus. Not only can we dwell in Him, in His perfect house, He will dwell in us. *"I will dwell in them and walk in them, I will be their God, and they shall be My people."* 2 Corinthians 6:16. (KJV) Just as we can move around in the House of Jesus, He can move around in us. He will dwell in us and walk in us. When that happens, it is hard for our enemy to cause us to fall. He must go through a triple security system to do it and Jesus will only let him have success to the effect that we will not be spoiled. Jesus is constantly patrolling the grounds of our home when He is within. Not one dart of the enemy can destroy us while under His protection. *"There hath no temptation taken you, but such as is common to man: but God is faithful, who will not suffer you to be tempted above that ye are able; but will with the temptation also make a way to escape, that ye may be able to bear it."* 1 Corinthians 10:13. (KJV) What a wonderful promise. In Jesus' House there is escape from every temptation. Jesus reinforced this in what is called "The Lord's Prayer." *"Lead us not into temptation but deliver us from evil."* What a house. The house is solid. It has a solid foundation. It is built on the rock; Jesus Christ and that rock will not fail you. *"Be strong and of a good courage, fear not, nor be afraid of them: for the LORD thy God, he it is that doth go with thee; he will not fail thee, nor forsake thee."* Deuteronomy 31:6. (KJV)

The people who dwell in the House of Jesus are called righteous and upright. Listen to this. *"Surly the righteous shall give thanks to Your name; the upright shall dwell in Your presence."* Psalm 140:13. (LITV) Once within the House of Jesus we can walk in a perfect way. We can walk without sin if we are in Him. *"My eyes shall be on the faithful of the land, that they may dwell with me; He who walks in a perfect way."* Psalm 101:6. (LITV) Jesus also brings another safety feature to our houses. It is the Holy Spirit. He is working side by side with Jesus to battle against our foes. When we sense the presence of the Holy Spirit within us, we know Jesus is there too. *"By this we know that we abide in Him, and He in us, because He has given us His Spirit."* 1 John 4:13. (EMTV) And lastly, Jesus will let us help Him build our house into the perfect place for both of us to dwell. *"We are workers together for God. And you are like a farm that belongs to God: You are a house that belongs to Him. Like an expert builder I built the foundation of that house. I used the gift that God gave me to do this. Others are building on that foundation. But everyone should be careful how he builds. The foundation has already been built. No one can build any other foundation. The foundation that has already been laid is Jesus Christ. Anyone can build on that foundation, using gold, silver, jewels, wood, grass, or straw. But the work that each person does will be clearly seen, because the day will make it plain. That Day will appear with fire, and the fire will test every man's work. If the building that a man puts on the foundation still stands after the fire, he will get his reward. But if his building is burned up, he will suffer loss."* 1 Corinthians 3:9-14. (MV)This is not the million-dollar question, it is the one that will determine your eternal destiny. How are you building your house? Are you trying to build it on your own? Do not strike another blow with the hammer without Jesus! Do not saw another board, without your Lord! Do not order any more supplies without seeking His guidance! And be sure and get some good rest this evening before you start tomorrow with Him!

We can go to sleep tonight, secure in the House-Jesus Christ, and receive the most peaceful sleep ever. *"I will both lay down in peace, and sleep: for you, LORD, only make me to dwell in safety."* Psalm 4:8. (MV) Do you suffer from insomnia? Do you have trouble sleeping? Enter the house of Jesus tonight and find rest.

Proverbs 3:24

"When you lie down, you will not be afraid: yes, you will lie down, and your sleep will be sweet."

Day Eighteen

Hello again. It is time to enter another chapter in this journal. I trust you had sweet sleep last evening. I had some vivid dreams, but they were not bad ones. As I was talking to Jesus about this entry, He brought the word, time to mind. Here on planet earth, we are driven by time. We go to sleep in time, we wake up in time. We go about our daily activities in time. We set appointments and make or break them, all in time. God on the other hand transcends time. He is above and beyond it. He was the one that created it for us. Since we are in time, He comes and meets us in time. The commandments tell us that He reserves one day of our time for Himself. Many of us give at least a portion of that time to Him. Since God is not limited by time however, we often do not understand Him or how He works. Let me give you an example. When it comes to prayer, does God need to answer our prayer in our time or His? Have you ever lost something? Have you ever prayed that you find it? I lost my cell phone a couple of days ago. I prayed that I would find it. In my mind, I felt the sooner I found it the better would be my chances of finding it. I felt the longer the time elapsed while it was out of my hand, the greater the chance of someone else running across it and doing whatever. A cell phone can contain a lot of personal information. Mine records the last 20 calls I made, the last 20 calls I received and the last 20 calls I missed. A person could find out a lot about someone with 60 calls to consider. So, I was praying. After the prayer, the answer came.

"Your cell phone is at the customer service desk in the mall, Donielle. You put it down when you had them send off that fax for you." I did not follow the voice though. I looked all over the truck. I did not find it. I went back to the last place where I thought I had it. We were in a mall eating some food. I went back to the chair where I last placed the bag containing the item I had purchased earlier. I looked on all the chairs by that table. I looked under the table and at the people around the table to see if any looked suspicious. It was not there.

In my mind, I went back to the last place I had been before I sat at the table. Jesus had assured me that would be where my cell phone was. He told me that before I even went to the table. He told me where to find it the very moment I realized it was not with me. My inner mind knew it was at the information desk, but I still stopped at the table. I still looked all over inside the truck. I ask myself why? Why couldn't I go with His instruction? Why didn't I trust His voice? I went to the desk and the lady smiled.

"You are looking for your cell phone, aren't you?

"Yes!" I replied. She handed it to me and when I passed by our friends, they told me I was lucky. It was not luck. It was an answer to prayer. How should we pray then to a God who transcends time? This God knows all about us. He knows what we are going to pray for before we ever pray for it. He knew I was going to pray that prayer six thousand years before I prayed it. He knew of that prayer before the world was created. Don't you think that if God had over six thousand years to answer that prayer, He just might be powerful enough to make provisions to answer that prayer no matter how much time has passed since I lost the item? What is my fifteen minutes compared to God's eternity? The moral of the story is this. If you feel it is too late to pray for something, it might be, but then again, it might not be, because maybe, just maybe our God is big enough, kind enough, loving enough to have made provision to answer your prayer long before you prayed it. Sometimes it is too late to have a prayer answered the way you would like it to be answered. But every prayer is answered. Some with yes, some with no and some with wait awhile. A God that transcends time really knows more about the whys and why nots than we do.

There is another aspect to timing in prayer. As I think about this, who was it that reminded me that the cell phone was not with me? It was Jesus of course. Since He knows the future, He knows when it is too late for me to go back to the place where I left it. If I am open to His voice, if I listen to His instruction, I will follow His prompting and arrive back to my phone before the other person takes it. He will give me enough time to do that because He knows when the other will come before they take it. That is why we need to have our ears tuned to His voice. If we lost something, if we went back too late to get it, chances are we did not hear His voice telling us within the proper time to retrieve what was lost. Perhaps we were engaged in an occupation that kept our mind from being open to Jesus. Perhaps the radio or television was going, and we were so caught up in it the sound of a still, small voice was drowned out. Perhaps we heard clear warnings, clear instructions but blatantly chose to not obey. Today as you go about your activities. Keep your mind open to the instruction of your Redeemer. He can save you a lot of time because He transcends time. He can make your schedule much more efficient because He knows what will come up way ahead of time. If you are tuned into His voice on your way to work, if there is a traffic problem or some delay ahead, He can and will suggest alternate routes to get somewhere. I learned about this the hard way.

Before receiving my speeding ticket, the Lord gave me numerous warnings to help me prevent it. It started a week or so before the fateful day.

"Donielle, This year when you and your partner go anywhere together, it would probably be better if you let him drive."

"Okay, Lord," I replied. "That sounds good to me. I often get spaced out while driving and he would be the more careful driver." Plus, it would give me more personal one on one time with Jesus. So, for the next few days whenever we went anywhere together, I let him drive. Then came the day of the ticket. The Lord gave me several warnings, but I was not listening. Before I ever got to my partners house, He tried to warn me again.

"Your son is bigger than you are, Donielle. He is not comfortable with riding in the middle. You could ride there much better." I did not pay attention. My son slid over in the middle and my partner came over to the driver's door expecting me to get out so he could drive. He waited there for a moment then went around to the passenger door and got in. Time was winding down now.

"Donielle, When you go to Chelan today go on the east side of the river." I heard His voice that time. So, I asked Martin, my partner.

"What side of the river should we go to Chelan on? Should we go on the east side or the west?"

"The east side seems to be just as fast." He replied. "But it really doesn't make much difference." As I drove toward the area where the bridge crosses the river, I had every intention of going on the east side. I was in the east lane. The light was red at the intersection and while they were waiting for it to turn green, Jesus spoke to me one more time, but I still did not listen.

"*Go straight, today, Donielle.*" I turned and went over the bridge. But still He warned me. When I came to the area where the speed limit drops from 60 mph to 50 mph, He spoke again.

"*Remember to slow down to 50 here Donielle.*" And I did. As I passed through the little town where the speed limit drops from 50 mph to 40 mph, He warned me again.

"*See that speed limit sign, Donielle. It says 40 mph. You need to slow down.*" I saw it and slowed down. I looked at my speedometer and I slowed down to 42 mph. But as I looked ahead, about a hundred yards or so there was a sign that read 60 mph. It was in sight. I stepped on it and the red and blue flashing lights came on. Whose fault was it that I got that ticket? The Lord had given me ample warnings. And so, He will with you if you listen for His voice. Sometimes people blame God for accidents that happen. Chances are good that before the accident, God gave them ample warnings but since they were not in the habit of listening to His voice, the warnings were not obeyed. We had the same pastor for nine years at one church we attended. There is one sermon he preached that stands out in my mind. Success is following the last words of Jesus. There are two definitions of success. We view success on whether a person or family are living the American Dream. Do they have a big house? Do they have new cars? Do they go on expensive vacations? Are they making lots of money? God's definition of success is quite a bit different. The questions He ask are these. *Did they do what I asked them to do yesterday? Are they doing what I am asking them to do today? Will they do what I ask them to do tomorrow.* If you will do whatever it was Jesus asked you to do last, you will be successful in God's terms, this God who is above time. He knows the end from the beginning. He knows what is best for us and will let us know about it. All we must do is listen and obey.

Hebrews 3:15

"Today if you will hear His voice," (obey, close not your ears but follow His instruction.) Emphasis supplied

Day Nineteen

It is another day at least on this end of the computer. Think back over yesterday for a little while. Did you hear your Lord speaking to you? Did you hear that still, small voice? Did you hear Him speaking to you through nature? Did you hear Him coming through the scriptures as you read your Bible? Were there any personal experiences you had during the day where He used someone else to speak to you? Is He in control of your life and sometimes you hear Him speaking to others through you? There are times in life when we go through periods of what might be termed: Dry Times. These are times when we have no evidence from the outside that Jesus is working in our life. His voice is unusually quiet, or we seem unable to tune in. Our emotions are neither high nor low. Our Christian walk is not on the mountain top and it is not in the valley but somewhere in-between. When these times come, there is possibly something between our soul and the Savior but not always. I found out today where in one area of my life, self was still exerting itself. When Jesus brought it to my attention, I yielded it to Him, and a sense of His presence returned. I would like to talk a little about what to do in dry times. If such a time comes to you and you want to return to those times when His peace that passes all understanding comes, then perhaps some of these steps can help.

1. Understand what kind of God we serve. Though He hates the sin, He loves the sinner. Though we slip and fall, His grace and mercy enable us to get up and start over. There will come a day when it is too late to return to Him but for most of us that time has not come yet. He is still there beside us waiting for us to turn to Him with all our heart. It might take a few minutes or several hours to remove all the things that are separating us from Jesus, but we have the assurance if we persist, we will eventually break through. Some people, and perhaps you, by now have let Jesus wake you up early enough in the morning to devote enough time with Him to be sure all of self is on the cross and all of Christ is on the throne of the heart. Here is a promise to start this process of coming back if you are feeling separated from Jesus. *"But some will come to me–those the Father has given me–and I will never, never reject them."* John 6:37. (MV)

2. Be truthful with yourself. Have you ever lied to yourself? Some people believe if they keep saying something about themselves it will eventually be true. They try to convince themselves it is true. Being truthful about ourselves, our weaknesses, our shortcomings is hard to do at times, but it is good for the soul. Another word that fits in here is confession. We need to confess our faults to Jesus. Tell Him about our weaknesses and ask for His strength to

strengthen them. He knows all about us. If we are lying to ourselves, we are also lying to God. Here are a couple of promises about confession we can claim. "*If we confess our sins, he is faithful and just and will forgive us our sins and purify us from all unrighteousness.*" 1 John 1:9. (NIV) Sometimes we have wronged a brother or sister and we need to make things right with them. First, we confess our wrong to Jesus then be open to His leading as we go to the one, we have wronged. Once things are right with other, we can again come to Jesus and be whole again. "*Therefore, confess your sins to each other and pray for each other so that you may be healed. The prayer of a righteousness man is powerful and effective.* James 5:16. (NIV)

3. Ask forgiveness. Jesus took your sin and mine and bore it on the cross. The weight of our sins was so heavy, it crushed Him. He paid the price. Sometimes we need to ask His forgiveness and start over again. If we have wronged someone, we need to not only confess our mistake to them but seek their forgiveness. If you know of someone who is burdened with sin and you also feel they are not able to come to Jesus to have their sin problem taken care of, you can pray the prayer of Jesus for them. It was a prayer for all of us, those of us who realized we had sinned and those who did not realize it or were lying to themselves, justifying themselves for their actions. Here it is. Pray this prayer for those you have a burden for and let Jesus take care of their sin problem. Once their sin is taken care of, He can come in with the

Holy Spirit and start a new work in them. *"Then said Jesus, Father, forgive them; for they know not what they do."* Luke 23:34. (KJV)

4. Decide in your life with the help of Jesus to forsake sin forever. If we persist in holding on to cherished sins, those sins will not only keep us separated from Jesus but will ultimately mean our eternal destruction. As much as Jesus loves us, if we persist in having our own way, He will ultimately let us go and leave us to the path we have chosen. Though it wrenches His heart there is nothing else He can do. *"Oh, how can I give you up, my Ephraim? How can I let you go? How can I forsake you like Admah and Zeboiim? My heart cries out within me; how I long to help you.* Hosea 11:8. (LB) Jesus wants us to be one with Him more than anything else. He has made every provision necessary for this. But still the choice is ours. *"Now that you are whole again: sin no more."* John 5:14. (LB)

5. If you still feel alienated from Jesus after following the above four suggestions, go to a room where you can be alone. Turn off all the noise in the room. Shut the door. There should be no distractions. Take a Bible with you and open it to God. You can pray a prayer like this. "Dear Jesus. Somehow, I do not feel I am as close to you as you would like me to be. I know you are an understanding God. You know why I am where I am. I have been truthful to you and myself. I have confessed my sins and have received the promise of your forgiveness. I have determined to forsake

my sins and follow you. I realize I cannot do this on my own, but you are longing to help me. I know your heart is crying out. 'How I long to help you.' I need your help. I need you to reveal to me if there is anything that is separating me from You. I have tried to listen for your voice but somehow am not able to hear it. Your Word is full of messages from You. I need to hear you speaking to me from this Bible. I plan to read from Psalms, but if there is any special instruction You have for me elsewhere in the Bible, lead me to it. Let me know that you are there, waiting, longing to communicate with me. Hear my prayer, Jesus. In Your name I ask this. Amen", Now open the word and read. Come as a child to a parent, a student to a teacher, sincerely seeking the wisdom that comes from Him. *"If any of you lacks wisdom, he should ask God, who gives generously to all without resenting it, and it will be given to him. But when he asks, he must believe and not doubt, because he who doubts is like a wave of the sea, blown and tossed by the wind.* James 1:5-6. (NIV)

In your reading, Jesus may bring something to your mind that is separating you from Him. If He does, yield it up to Him, let Him remove it from you. It is not worth keeping if it is separating you from Him. You will need to have it removed if you plan on spending eternity with Him. Decide now. Is it worth losing out on eternal life for? Give it up. Let Jesus have it then follow His leading as He brings you back. This may be one of the hardest things you have to do. The sin might be so entrenched in your soul, part of you will have to be cut away. Surgery usually comes with pain but in the end, healing and wholeness can and will come and you will have peace. There are some sins though that you must never confess to others. There are some weaknesses that are handled between you and your Savior alone. No ear needs to hear but His. If you are having trouble accepting God's forgiveness for these sins, step out in faith. Take Him at His word. Ask for wisdom again to transform your mind so the guilt will be borne by Jesus. You need not wear it a moment longer. It is the enemy who is our accuser. If some sin of yours will cause another to stumble, Jesus will know what the other can take and counsel you. His counsel may go something like this though. When the woman taken in adultery was the only one left at the feet of Jesus, here is what He told her. "*Woman, where are they? Has no one condemned you?' She said, 'No one, Lord.' And Jesus said, 'Neither do I condemn you; go and do not sin again.'*"John 8:10-11. (NIV)

Before you march off to confess a sin to someone you feel guilty to, be sure and seek wisdom from Jesus first. Make sure it is what He wants you to do. Sometimes it is necessary and leads to reconciliation, but there are also times when just the opposite happens. Perhaps the other person is not under the control of the Holy Spirit. A confession out of line to such can cause discouragement and lead to the ruin of a friendship, not build it up. If you have been involved in sins of impurity, mentioning those sins to others can cause their unsanctified imagination to conquer up images that will forever influence the way they look at you. Seek God please! Consider the final Bible text on this entry before sharing any of your past sins with others.

Our time today is up now. But your time with Jesus is not. Take Him with you whether it is morning when you read this, noon, night or somewhere in-between. He loves you; you know!

Philippians 4:8

"Finally, brethren, whatsoever things are true, whatsoever things are honest, whatsoever things are just, whatsoever things are pure, whatsoever things are lovely, whatsoever things are of good report; if there be any virtue, and if there be any praise, think on these things."

Day Twenty

Well, two thirds of our time together have passed. There is only a third to go. Just ten more days. If it takes twenty to thirty days to establish a new habit, hopefully you are close to establishing a habit of keeping your mind focused on the fact that Jesus is at your right hand, leading and guiding in your life. You could be establishing the habit of turning to Him at least ten percent of your waking time, or six minutes out of every hour. You could be forming a habit of hearing His voice speaking to you more and more clearly. You could be forming the habit of allowing Jesus to wake you and reading from your Bible daily, drinking from the springs of living water, or setting at the feet of Jesus. You could be in the habit of allowing Him to send you on Divine appointments where your faith is strengthened as you see how He is working–not only in your life–but the lives of those He sends you to. You could be forming the habit of sinning less, of depending upon yourself less and depending on Jesus more. Your mind could be forming the habit of keeping a good, Christian song playing in the background to help keep your thoughts stayed on Him. You could also be experiencing love in a stronger way than you ever have before. *"By this shall all men* *know that ye are my disciples, if ye have love one to another."* John 13:36. (KJV) Perhaps we can focus on love a little bit today.

A few years ago, I unwisely went into partnership with an unbeliever. Things went good for a while but in time the true nature of each of us came out. I was the Christian and longsuffering. I tried to represent Christ as much as I could. I gave and gave and gave but he was never satisfied. I justified myself in saying that I had done all I could to live the gospel. I will follow the advice I gave in the closing text yesterday and not dwell on the unlovely things that developed. When all was said and done, I had an enemy. I do not know how many of you have had enemies, but it is not fun. In the closing days of our partnership, I could sense his hatred, I could feel his bitterness. In and of myself, I could not find love for him in my heart. The experience was so depressing, I even requested that my membership be dropped from the church. I felt if I had an enemy who hated me so much, I was not fit to be a Christian. Satan came in and muddied my mind. It took a while to let the blood-stained banner of Jesus cover my discouragement and bring hope again. When I finally turned the situation completely over to Jesus, He took care of it very quietly and simply. I had born the burden for nearly two years before I sought His solution and once yielded, He took care of the problem very quickly. I ask myself the question now. Did this individual see the love of Jesus in me? *"By this shall all men know that ye are my disciples, if ye have love one to another."*

*I*t is hard to love the unlovely. It is humanly impossible in many respects. All true love comes from Jesus. Do you have any enemies? Do you love them? What did Jesus tell us? *"But I say unto you, Love your enemies, bless them that curse you, do good to them that hate you, and pray for them which despitefully use you, and persecute you; That ye may be the children of your Father which is in heaven: for He maketh his sun to rise on the evil and on the good, and sendeth rain on the just and on the unjust."* Matthew 5:44-45. (KJV) How do we bless someone that curses us? I did what I felt was a lot of good to my enemy. I prayed and continue to pray for him. How do we bless someone? Evidently to bless someone is part of the process we use to show the love of Jesus toward them. I suppose we could give them something. I blessed him with gifts, food, extra money, tools. I even gave him a vehicle to use in place of the one he used that only got two or three miles to the gallon. As I search out these questions, I can only come up with one answer. The love Jesus is talking about here does not come from us, it comes from Him. It is His love that others will see in us. The only way they will see that love in us though is if Jesus is in us because if Jesus is not in us, then His love is not in us. When others meet you, do they see yourself or Jesus? Can the world see Jesus in you?

Love is a gift. It is one of the fruits of the Spirit. It comes to us when we have the Spirit of Jesus in us. It comes to us for our enemies, our friends, and our families. When people see the person, who has his life hid in Jesus, they will see Jesus. *"When they saw the courage of Peter and John and realized that they were unschooled, ordinary men, they were astonished, and they took note that these men had been with Jesus.* Acts 4:13. (NIV) If Jesus is becoming a strong persona in your life, you should be noticing that you have more love and tolerance for those around you. Earlier in this journal I mentioned the book by Brother Lawrence. There was another minister who followed the practice of the presence of Christ in his life. He also wrote a journal. I would like to include a few of his entries here for your consideration. The pastors name was Frank Laubach. Born in the United States in 1884, he was a missionary to the illiterate, teaching them to read so they could know the beauty of the Scriptures. Here is what started the process in his life. One day he asks himself these questions.

"Can we have that contact with God all the time? All the time awake, fall asleep in His arms, and awaken in His presence? Can we do his will all the time? Can we think His thoughts all the time? Can I bring the Lord back in my mind-flow every few seconds so that God shall always be in my mind? I choose to make the rest of my life an experiment in answering this question." He started this experiment in January of 1930. By the 26th he made the next entry.

"I am feeling God in each movement, by an act of will–willing that He shall direct these fingers that now strike this typewriter–willing that He shall pour through my steps as I walk."

"March 1, 1930: This sense of being led by an unseen hand which takes mine while another hand reaches ahead and prepares the way, grows upon me daily... sometimes it requires a long time early in the morning. I determine not to get out of bed until that mind set upon the Lord is settled.

"April 18, 1930: I have tasted a thrill in fellowship with God which has made anything discordant with God, disgusting. This afternoon the possession of God has caught me up with such sheer joy that I thought I never had known anything like it. God was so close and so amazingly lovely that I felt like melting all over with a strange, blissful contentment. Having had this experience, which comes to me now several times a week, the thrill of filth repels me, for I know its power to drag me from God. And after an hour of close friendship with God my soul feels clean, as new fallen snow."

"May 14, 1930: Oh, this thing of keeping in constant touch with God, of making Him the object of my thought and the companion of my conversations, is the most amazing thing I ever ran across. It is working. I cannot do it even half of the day–not yet, but I believe I shall be doing it some day for the entire day. It is a matter of acquiring a new habit of thought."

"May 24, 1930: This concentration upon God is strenuous, but everything else has ceased to be so. I think more clearly, I forget less frequently. Things which I did with a strain before, I now do easily and with no effort whatever. I worry about nothing and lose no sleep. I walk on air a good part of the time. Even the mirror reveals a new light in my eyes and face. I no longer feel in a hurry about anything. Everything goes right. Each minute I meet calmly as though it were not important. Nothing can go wrong except one thing. That is, God may slip from my mind."

June 1, 1930: Ah, God, what a new nearness this brings for Thee and me, to realize that Thou alone canst understand me, for thou alone knowest all! Thou art no longer a stranger, God! Thou art the only being in the universe who is not partly a stranger! Thou art all the way inside with me–here. . . I mean to struggle tonight and tomorrow as never before, not once to dismiss thee. For when I lose Thee for an hour I lose. The thing thou wouldst do can only be done when thou hast full sway all the time."

"Last Monday was the most successful day of my life to date, so far as giving my day in complete and continuous surrender to God is concerned. . . I remember how I looked at people with a love God gave, they looked back and acted as though they wanted to go with me. I felt then that for a day I saw a little of that marvelous pull that Jesus had as He walked along the road day after day 'God-intoxicated' and radiant with the endless communion of His soul with God."

Is such a goal attainable? For Frank it was, and for us it can be. Did you see after a few months in living as if in the presence of Jesus that His love came in and took possession of Frank? And when he met others, they sensed the drawing power of that love. *"They took note of them that they had been with Jesus."* Acts 4:13. (KJV) There is a short text in the Bible. It is only three words, but it is a goal for us to try and attain. It is what we have been talking about for the last twenty days. It is what Frank developed in his life. He learned to keep in contact with Jesus 24/7, without ceasing. This text is a promise. We can claim this promise and watch and see how Jesus goes to work to fulfill this promise in our lives. Are you ready for this text? You have heard it before but probably understand it now more than 99.999 percent of the people out there. You know what it means by now and are beginning to experience it in own your life. *"Pray without ceasing."* 1 Thessalonians 5:17. (KJV)

If you have not yet established the habits mention at the start of this entry, do not give up. It took Frank Laubach several months. But the rewards of seeking after Jesus are well worth the effort. Wherever you are now. Try Frank's experiment in your own life. If it takes the rest of your life to attain this continual Pearl of Friendship with Jesus, make the rest of your life a quest, an experiment to have Him fully possess you, He in you and you in Him.

Romans 8:38-39

"For I am persuaded, that neither death, nor life, nor angels, nor principalities, nor powers, nor things present, nor things to come, nor height, nor depth, nor any other creature, shall be able to separate us from the love of God, which is in Christ Jesus our Lord."

Day Twenty-One

Good afternoon, or is it morning? This is the last day of our third week together if you are reading one entry per day. How are you? How are you and Jesus doing? There was a season of time when I heard the voice of Jesus quite distinctly today. He informed me that in my business I must be crystal clear. Everything must be upright and without fault. Do you realize how hard that is going to be? Everything transparent with no blemishes. There are very few businesses that can make that claim. It is a tall order. If I had to do it alone, it would be impossible. But my partner, Jesus can make it happen. Have you ever thought about forming a partnership with Jesus before? It has a lot of advantages. Jesus is the owner of this world even though Satan claims it as his own. Jesus owns mega-trillions in real estate holdings. He has more money than the largest banks in the world. What a silent partner He makes. He does not want to be a silent partner though; He wants to be quite vocal and have His say on how things are to be done. He knows all about the very people who I will go to give estimates to. He knows what it will take to sell them on our services. He is a very honest partner too. He will never cheat me.

He is a great bookkeeper. In Heaven, He keeps the books in order, the Book of Life, The Book of Records along with a Book of Death. He is the Creator of all nature and since I am in the landscape business–the business of creating beautiful landscapes–we have that in common. He was the greatest teacher of all time so He can teach my employees to be the most efficient workers. He can keep my plants alive. He who spoke trees into existence can surely keep them alive. Do you understand how mechanical He is? He holds worlds in space, the universe is kept in sync right to the hundredth milli-second. What is our equipment to such a genius? He can fix anything.

In a book I read a few years ago one of Jesus' warriors ran out of gas several miles away from home. The wind chill factor was below zero. There was no one around for miles. This servant/ partner with Jesus opened the problem to his Lord and after dying and stopping, the car started up again. It made it all the way to his home and died in the driveway. He checked the mileage he got on that trip and a bunch of other stuff and it was true. Jesus made the car run on angel power or Divine Petroleum. What an awesome partner Jesus was to this man and what an awesome partner He can be to each one of us.

In another story, Jesus intervened in a remarkable way to save a college student's life or at least from serious harm. She was a pretty girl and worked evenings at a mall to help pay her way through college. One winter evening, as she headed out to her car, she saw a group of guys not far from it. The mall required the employees to park far on the outer edges of the parking lot so the customers could be closer for more convenient shopping. Just a few parking spaces over from her car was a van. As she headed toward her car, a fear came over her. She knew something was wrong. She sent up a prayer to Jesus. The guys watched her. They must have known she worked late. She got in her car, turned the key, and drove by them. One of the guys ran toward her and hollered.

"You can't drive that car! It is impossible." She waved at him and went home. The guys ran to their van and tried to follow her home, but it would not start. She drove to her apartment and parked the car in her garage. The next morning when she went out to drive to college, her car would not start. She knew a little about mechanics so opened the hood to see what was wrong with it. There was no battery. Someone had cut the cables and removed it. She assumed it was the guys in the van. She was able to give a description to the police later and they apprehended some of them. What a mechanic Jesus is! He can make cars run on Divine Petroleum and start with Divine Battery Power. Jesus shared with me that if I can make my business transparent, without fault through His power, He would bless me. Just what that blessing means, I do not know, nor do

I care. Any blessing from Jesus must be a great blessing. *"Beloved, I wish above all things that thou mayest prosper and be in health, even as thy soul prospereth."* 3 John 1:2. (KJV)

How is your soul prospering? How is your spiritual life doing? Are you in good health? For several months now, I have been given little warnings from my partner, Jesus about minding my health. I need to eat the right foods. I need to keep nourishment up with good vitamins and a healthy diet. I eat too much sugar. If my soul is going to prosper and be transparent, I will need to bring my diet in the natural order of creation. Thankfully, my wife is planning to do this also. We tried it for a while a couple of years ago. I do not have a lot of weight on my bones. I lost 13 pounds. I got down to under 165 pounds and I am supposed to be 6'3 according to army measurements. I later went on a weight gaining program with strength training and got up to 190 pounds. I looked better at that weight. More fat makes for fewer wrinkles and at fifty something, wrinkles are permanently etched all over my face. Most people have the opposite problem. They want to lose weight. I had to gain it. There is even a promise in the Bible that mentions how I can keep from getting skinny. He can make my bones fat. The promise holds a lot of good counsel so I will print it all out for your enjoyment.

"Is not this the fast that I have chosen? to lose the bands of wickedness, to undo the heavy burdens, and to let the oppressed go free, and that

*ye break every yoke? Is it not to deal thy bread to the hungry, and that thou bring the poor that are cast out to thy house? when thou seest the naked, that thou cover him; and that thou hide not thyself from thine own flesh? Then shall thy light break forth as the morning, and thine health shall spring forth speedily: and thy righteousness shall go before thee; the glory of the LORD shall be thy rereward. Then shalt thou call, and the LORD shall answer; thou shalt cry, and he shall say, Here I am. If thou take away from the midst of thee the yoke, the putting forth of the finger, and speaking vanity; And if thou draw out thy soul to the hungry, and satisfy the afflicted soul; then shall thy light rise in obscurity, and thy darkness be as the noon day: And the LORD shall guide thee continually, and satisfy thy soul in drought, **and make fat thy bones**: and thou shalt be like a watered garden, and like a spring of water, whose waters fail not. And they that shall be of thee shall build the old waste places: thou shalt raise up the foundations of many generations; and thou shalt be called, The repairer of the breach, The restorer of paths to dwell in."* Isaiah 58:6-12. (KJV)

Fantastic promises especially for a landscaper. Build up the old waste places, repairer of the breach, continual guidance from my partner, Jesus, watered gardens with springs of water, whose waters fail not. There is even promise of great health. *"And thine health shall spring forth speedily."* Remember the transparent business He wanted me to make. *"And thy righteousness shall go before thee; and the glory of the Lord shall be thy rereward.*" And finally, the promise of calling on the Lord and He shall answer me! There is another text in the Bible that talks about fat bones. Here it is in Proverbs 15:29-30. (KJV) "*The LORD is far from the wicked: but he heareth the prayer of the righteous. The light of the eyes rejoiceth the heart: and a good report maketh the bones fat.*" A good report. That is what the Lord wants people to say about my business. If they give a good report about it, I will have plenty of work. There will be income enough so I will not want for anything. And again, the Lord will hear me when I make a request of Him. A transparent business, a transparent soul, spotless, without blemish. Have Thine own way Lord, have Thine own way. Think about what kind of a partner Jesus will make for you in whatever endeavor you choose or are doing now. Let Jesus make your life transparent and your soul crystal clear.

Joshua 1:8

"This book of the law shall not depart out of thy mouth; but thou shalt meditate therein day and night, that thou mayest observe to do according to all that is written therein: for then thou shalt make thy way prosperous, and then thou shalt have good success."

Day Twenty-Two

It is another day. I hope you are going through this book one day at a time instead of reading it through once and trying to put the Spirit of Christ to work in you for the next thirty days. By reading this over day by day for thirty days, the concept of turning to Jesus constantly can be reinforced. The mind needs to be reminded or our enemy will surely bring in all kinds of things to keep us from relating to Jesus in an hour-by-hour way. It is spring here in Washington and more and more work is coming in. I get up early and go to bed late. It takes time to write these thoughts down, so it was good to get started earlier in the year before all the work came in. There is just eight days left. I have missed a couple of days and you might also but try not to miss too many in a row. I hope you are finding this interesting and informative. Before I write, I spend time talking to Jesus so that my mind can provide a clear channel for Him to speak. The last few days, a thought kept running through my mind, so I talked to Jesus about it. Let us start out with a Bible text so you can see what we will be talking about for a paragraph or two. *"Therefore, if any man be in Christ, he is a new creature: old things are passed away; behold, all things are become new."* 2Corinthians 5:17. (KJV)

I talked with my friend about what it means to be in Him. To be in Jesus in the truest sense of the word, we would be in constant communion with Him. He would be guiding us on a moment-by-moment bases, and we would be responding, obeying, communicating, praising Him or any other form of living that brings glory to God. When the sap is running in the vine or the trees, it is constantly running, it never stops. The roots bring moisture up to the leaves. The leaves combine it with light and create sugar to send back down to nourish the roots so they can grow and produce more roots. When Christ referred to Himself as the Vine and we His branches, this type of constantly drawing and giving is implied. When we truly are in Christ the old things are died. We are a brand-new creation. Sin no longer has sway over us. Christ have us completely covered inside and out. But suppose I forgot Jesus for a block of three hours. Would I still be in Him during that time when I am not consciously reminding myself of His presence? What would happen to the vine if for three hours there was no fluid running through its system? Newly planted plants often wilt and some die when there is not enough fluid within them to keep up the supply they need. What is the vine like in the winter? It is alive but the sap is not flowing. It does not have leaves. The branches are not nurturing the roots neither are the roots supporting the branches. Since there are no leaves, there is no fruit. I will venture to say if we forget Jesus for long blocks of time, we are not in Christ during a portion of that time. For example, a flower can look fresh for quite a while after it is cut from the plant. If it is put in water, it will continue to draw fluid but eventually will die. Likewise, the old man of sin will crop up when we are separated from Christ for blocks of time. Last Sunday I had forgotten about Jesus for about two hours and I thought I was doing fine. I felt that I was in Him and He in me even though the communication lines were not open between us. Then something happened and part of my old nature sprang to the front very quickly. I got angry. I could feel it surging over me. Then I remembered Jesus and quickly opened the communication lines again and He brought it back into control for me before it had a chance to bear fruit.

While we are in Christ, old things are died, all things are new. Jesus is there with new life straight from the Throne of God. Our spiritual nature is alive and well. We are doing what God ordained us to do during that time. When we forget Him though for blocks of over two or three hours, then we are more susceptible to the temptations of our enemy. After three hours away from Christ, we could very well be back into the old body of death. If we forget Him for a day, we become dehydrated. The wellspring of living water that keeps us on the road to everlasting life begins to dry up and we soon find ourselves walking in darkness. The Sun of Righteousness is not shining in us and through us. If we forget Jesus for two days, while we are away from Christ, Satan starts to draw a cloak of darkness over us. It is so dense that it is highly effective in blocking out the rays of glory that come streaming down from our Father. Most of us have been as much as a week or longer away from meaningful communion with Jesus. We ultimately die spiritually. That is why when we get back with Jesus, we are a new creature. He must create our spiritual nature all over again. Here is another text that might clear things up a little more.

"I know I am rotten through and through so far as my old sinful nature is concerned. No matter which way I turn, I cannot make myself do right. I want to, but I cannot. When I want to do good, I do not. And when I try not to do wrong, I do it anyway. But if I am doing what I do not want to do, I am not really the one doing it, the sin within me is doing it. It seems to be a fact of life that when I want to do what is right, I inevitably do what is wrong. I love God's law with all my heart. But there is another law at work within me that is at war with my mind. This law wins the fight and makes me a slave to the sin that is still within me. Oh, what a miserable person I am! Who will free me from this life that is dominated by sin? Thank God! The answer is in Jesus Christ our Lord. So, you see how it is: In my mind I really want to obey God's law, but because of my sinful nature I am a slave to sin. Romans 7:18-25. (LB) Without that active, moment by moment conscious involvement with Jesus, our old nature comes back to haunt us. When we cut off the communication with our

Lord, we cut off His spiritual nature within us. It is no longer there to defeat the enemy. Since we were born in sin, our typical nature is sinful and when separated from Christ we have no choice over how we live. We can try all we want but sin has enslaved us. We will eventually die spiritually just like the plant that is separated from its roots. Only Jesus Christ, with us day by day, hour by hour, moment by moment has the power to deliver us and sustain us in our Christian walk.

There are millions and millions of well-meaning Christians who go to church every week. They are careful not to use bad language. They read their Bible. They study their Bible lesson. They say a blessing before each meal. They visit the sick. They stop and help a person in need along the road. They witness and may even give Bible studies. They pay a faithful tithe and give offerings of all their increase. They hold leadership positions in the church. They may teach, preach, walk, and talk the Word but if they are not in Christ on a consistent basis, they are dying or dead spiritually. They may know and keep all the doctrines they feel necessary for Salvation but if they are not in friendship with Jesus, they are walking in darkness. Just as we cannot live physically without the breath of life, He gave us upon conception, we cannot live spiritually without the breath of His Spirit entering us constantly. Prayer is our spiritual breath, and sad to say if we do not realize that we need it continually, we will not be in Christ for exceedingly long. He will not stay long where He is not invited. "*They act as if they are religious, while rejecting the power that makes them Godly.*" 2 Timothy 3:5. (NLT)

Many feels if they go to God in the morning and spend half an hour or more in private devotions, they are assured of His abiding presence all the rest of the day. There are others who feel they can go the whole week on an experience they had with Him on their day of worship. They do not have private worship at all. How can they expect to be in Christ? They go through the day without once giving Him a thought, but if you were to ask them if they are Christ followers they would say yes. They are not following Christ. They are following their own paths. Christ is the one following them. He is running after them, trying to catch a few moments of companionship with them. To follow someone, you need to be able to see them while they are ahead of you, leading the way. If you were in a car following a friend to some destination and did not keep your eyes on their car for long blocks of time, they would turn, and you would not see them go to the right or left. You would keep going straight. You would lose sight of them. When you realized they were no longer ahead of you, you could get out your cell phone and call them. They would tell you where they were. You would make the necessary corrections in your course and get back on track. Same it is with Jesus. If you have gone for a long block of time without talking with Him, He is most likely be lost to you. You need to call out to Him. He will tell you the needed corrections to make in your course to get back on track to your destination. Our destination is eternal life. We will be in the presence of Jesus for eternity. We need to practice His presence here so it will become part of our nature. If this happens here, we will be right at home with Him over there.

In closing this entry, I would like to share an experience that happened today while working. There were two crews on two separate jobs. The other crew needed the dump truck, so I was left with a trailer to haul rocks with. The trailer did not have side boards. After loading it up, I noticed that some of the rocks rocked back and forth. My ear was tuned to the inner guiding voice and the word came quite clearly.

"Donielle, you need to get some side boards for that trailer. You should make some before carrying to many more loads of rock. Since you do not have them made yet, you need to chain the larger rocks down and use the binders." I did what I was told. I had two chains and a strap with a wench on one end of it. I bound the loose rocks in place and started down the hill. At one point, the trailer hit a rut in the road and the large rock on the back shifted. It may well have bounced off the trailer and landed on the road, but the chain held it in place. I pulled over further up the road and readjusted the chain over the rock again. That evening just before dark, I made the side boards. Not only will they keep the rocks in, but they may also save me a large

fine for carrying an unsecured load. *"For a time is coming when people will no longer listen to right teaching. They will follow their own desires and will look for teachers who will tell them whatever they want to hear. They will reject the truth and follow strange myths. But you should keep a clear mind in every situation.* 2 Timothy 4:3-5. (NLT) The best way to keep a clear mind is to keep it focused on Jesus. We must do this in every situation, or we could very easily make costly mistakes in our lives. If our ear is tuned to His guidance, He will help us in everything we do.

Psalm 54:4

"But God is my helper. The Lord is the one who keeps me alive!"

Day Twenty-Three

It was another beautiful spring day today. We had perfect weather. The temperature hovered between 68 and 70 degrees. I enjoyed working in the yard. The flowers were very pretty. I stuck my nose down to many of the apple blossoms. Each had its own unique, fragrant smell. The cherry and pear were also in full bloom while the peaches and nectarines were just about gone. I spent time with the Creator, God. There is a small room I go to at times and pour out my heart. Though the weather was nice, I chose this room for a short time. While there my thoughts focused on storms for some reason. It must not have been a storm here but one somewhere else. Do you ever have questions you would like to ask God? I do. A lot of the questions focus on what the future will hold for me or for members of the church I attend. Questions about the future are not ones that Jesus answers for me often, though. I have tried to bring up some, but there is silence on the part of my Maker with many of them. *"My grace is sufficient for you, Donielle,"* He says. When I hear this, I am satisfied that He knows what is best. Today, however, a bit of the future was revealed. As I asked Him why the storm theme in my mind, some pictures came into my consciousness. I have been in some bad storms. I have watched as tornados passed overhead. I have seen the gray, green angry clouds and watched the lightning streak across the sky followed by the thunder. I have passed through snowstorms where I appeared to be surrounded by a tunnel of weather, dark and ominous. Once while traveling in the western portion of northern Oregon, we came out of what appeared to be a tunnel storm. The snow had come. Trains were stalled all along the tracks. Cars and trucks were strung in the ditches for miles while their occupants took shelter somewhere out of the cold. After the snow came the freezing rain. When we came out of this along near evening and saw the sun setting over the ocean, we breathed a sigh of relief. We made it. We had come from the darkness into the light. Looking back, we saw the blackness that swallowed up everything while before us was the sparkling ocean with a golden bridge across it.

As I talked to Jesus about the future, the picture that came to my mind was one of a white church with a tall steeple. Hundreds of people were coming out of that church. To the west, the sun shone brilliantly with that golden trail across the ocean. To the east was the dark, ominous blackness of a gathering storm. A chilly wind was blowing in from the clouds. A large shadow of darkness seemed to consume the land. I was outside the church, watching the unfolding events. Had I been with the people of that church, I would have gone to the east and headed across the golden bridge to the sun, but these people all headed for the storm. Not one of them turned back. The darkness of the storm surrounded them and then I was there with them struggling onward. While a large mass of people entered the storm, I noticed that the numbers pressing on were dwindling. Some were falling. Many were floundering around in the darkness. Their cries were drowned out by the shrieking wind. On we toiled against the darkness for what seemed a long time, though the picture came in a few moments. After a while, a little band of people emerged from the darkness. They were only a small percentage of those who had started. The words of a scripture text came to mind as we came out. *"Press on toward the mark for the prize of the high calling of God in Christ Jesus."* Philippians 3:14. I do not know why this picture entered my mind. I do not know what it means. Even as I state this here on the computer though, another text comes into my mind. *"For many are called, but few are chosen."* Matthew 22:14. (KJV) At this point in this entry I would like you to ask yourself a question. What am I willing to give up for Jesus?

For the last couple of years, I have been trying for one of the bigger commercial bids. A week or so ago I sent in a bid for landscaping the local high school and found out that not only was I the lowest bidder, but I was also the only landscape bidder. I thought it quite strange because usually there are no less than a dozen landscapers submitting bids for these jobs. I was quite happy to know that I had finally won a large bid. It would mean the final and complete elimination of every debt I owe and give some capital to purchase some much-needed equipment. When I checked into it though, I found the winning general contractor has stated the landscape portion of their contract would be self-performed. That meant that although I was the winning landscape bidder, they would not use me but do the work themselves. This did not make sense, since their company was nearly three hours driving time from the project. We were located about five miles from it. I complained a little to some of the workers and people around me, but finally came to terms. Then as I spent time with my Lord, the loss did not seem bad at all. I was content. Eventually the whole project loss diminished and became nothing to me. The future was in the hands of my Guiding Companion. He knew what was best.

A couple of days ago though I felt the prompt to call the contractor. I was surprised to find that we will probably be doing the work. The general's bids all came in over budget. A school board meeting has been called. As soon as the extra money is approved, the project will start. It does not matter to me now though. When it comes, we will move in and do it, but being with Jesus seems to be a lot more important to me than any contract no matter what size it is. What are you willing to give up for Jesus? I was asked, if Jesus called me to do some other line of work, would I be willing to leave my business with a large, profitable contract in the works? I would have to say, yes at this point. Whether that is something I will have to do or not, I do not really know, or do I feel bad about it. I will have a much brighter future with Jesus, a future that last not for the duration of a landscape project but forever. As for the debts I owe, *"For my God shall supply all your need according to his riches in glory by Christ Jesus.* Philippians 4:19. (KJV) *"He that loves his father or mother more than me is not worthy of me: and he that loves son or daughter more than me is not worthy of me. And whoever is not willing to take up his cross and follow me is not worthy of me. The one who finds his life shall lose it: and whoever loses his life for my sake shall find it."* Matthew 10:37-39. (RV)

My wife cannot understand this type of thinking. To her the security of a home, a job, and a retirement account is uppermost on her list of goals. When the storm comes, we all must enter it. We cannot outrun it. We cannot flee the opposite direction from whence it comes. We will all have to go through it. We cannot take our church building with us. We cannot take our home with us. We cannot take our job with us. We cannot take our security with us. All our possessions will have to be left behind. We must advance into the storm. It will eventually come and claim all we have worked for; all we have saved. We can only take the faith we have developed through Jesus, Christ our Lord with us as we press on toward the prize, of the mark, of the high calling of our God in Christ Jesus. What are you willing to give to Jesus? He requires your everything. Do you trust Him enough? Do you know that He knows best? Could you leave your son or daughter behind to follow Him? What about your mother or father? The storm is advancing. At your left hand is a cross. You need to take it up on your shoulder now. You will not have to bear it alone though. Jesus is at your right hand. He is holding out His yoke. *"Come unto me, all ye that labor and are heavy laden, and I will give you rest. Take my yoke upon you and learn of me; for I am meek and lowly in heart: and ye shall find rest unto your souls. For my yoke is easy, and my burden is light."* Matthew 11:28-30. (KJV) "Must Jesus bear the cross alone, and all the world goes free? No. There's a cross for everyone, and there's a cross for me." What is the cross we are called to bear? It is the surrender of yourself to God, day by day, moment by moment. At this point, all I can say is trust in Jesus. Take Him at His word.

Yoke up with Him and move toward the storm. It is better to be yoked up with Jesus in that storm than to be in it alone. When the darkness comes, He is the light. When the winds shriek around you, He is your peace. Your soul will be stilled as He cries out *"Peace! Be still!"* And you will know what manner of man this is that *"even the winds and waves obey Him."*

While driving back from Spokane, Washington a few weeks ago with my wife, we were listening to a music artist, Josh Groban. Some of you have probably heard him sing. I do not know if he is a follower of Christ but one of His songs struck us with a power that can only be attained by inspiration. That song is called "You Raise Me Up." I took the liberty to add some new words to the song. If you have heard it, you can follow along with the tune in your mind as you read.

YOU RAISE ME UP

When I am down, and oh my soul, so weary
When troubles come and my heart
burdened be
Then, I am still and wait here in the silence
Until You come, and sit a while with me

You raise me up, so I can stand on mountains
You raise me up, to walk on stormy seas
I am strong when I am on Your shoulders
You raise me up... To more than I can be

While I wait, the darkness gathers round me

Until You come, and brighten up my way
Then You speak, and give such words
of comfort
They raise me up, and carry me away

You raise me up, so I can stand on mountains
You raise me up, to walk on stormy seas
I am strong when I am on Your shoulders
You raise me up... To more than I can be

Someday soon, You'll show me that bright city
When with the saved, on heaven's shores
I'll stand
And there proclaim, throughout the
endless ages
The saving grace, of Jesus Christ the Lamb

You'll raise me up, far higher than
the mountains
Forever gone, will be those stormy seas
Then I'll lean, against my Savior's shoulders
Who raised me up...To more than I could be

I am strong when I am on Your shoulders
You raise me up... To more than I can be

Revised words by Donielle Ingersoll

Jesus is requesting of you today, *"Take My yoke upon you and learn of Me. My yoke is easy, My burden light. Come and find a rest for your soul."* He is waiting to raise you up so you can walk on the mountains. He longs to raise you up above the stormy seas. Like to Peter of old, He is holding out His hand. Won't you take it in your own?

Thank you, Reader. You will not regret this decision. See that scar where the rusty nail pierced Him? It was for you. See the holes where the thorns penetrated His brow? He wore that crown of thorns for you. See His feet? They were nailed to the cross that was meant for you. He took up your cross and mine. He carried it up the hill where they nailed Him to it. There stretched out between earth and heaven, the storm came. The darkness gathered around Him. He bore the complete brunt of that storm so you and I would not have to. Now He speaks peace to your soul and mine. Come, come to Jesus!

1 Peter 2:9

"You are a chosen people, a royal priesthood, a holy nation, a people belonging to God, that you may declare the praises of him who called you out of darkness into his wonderful light.

Day Twenty-Four

This is the first day of our last week together. Soon it will be Jesus and you. You must develop your own friendship with Him. My experience will not do. The experience of a pastor, a friend or a spouse will not do. You must find your own way to Him. Many of you are there with Him by your side, now. You know that your Redeemer lives, because He is living within you. For some He has marked out the path you are to travel. You are on that path now, following where He leads. For others, you know what He wants you to do but you have not allowed Him to lead you. You are not yet ready to relinquish control of your future to the one who knows the end from the beginning. For you, what more can I say? Why not "Taste and See?" Do you believe He knows what is best for you? Do you believe He knows what work for Him will make you the happiest? He is holding out a bright, everlasting future to you. This earth will pale in comparison to the eternal riches and glory of Jesus Christ. Jesus is a personal God. He wants to be your friend. Can you imagine looking into a face one day and finding it the face of Jesus? Can you imagine the love that shows from His eyes as He looks at you? Can you sense the awe you will feel when in His presence? This is the one who loves you with an everlasting love. He is the one who longs to gather you under His wings as a mother hen gathers her tiny chicks. Can you sense what it will be like when He wraps His arms around you and says, "Welcome home". If you are afraid to give total control of your life to Jesus, may I ask why? What do you fear? Perhaps you do not know how to surrender.

There is a small book that has sold millions and millions of copies. It is called "Steps to Christ." Many of you have read it but few of us can say we have practiced the instruction given there. Here is a portion of one chapter that gives us the method we need to follow in surrendering our will to Jesus.

"Many are inquiring, 'How am I to make the surrender of myself to God?' You desire to give yourself to Him, but you are weak in moral power, in slavery to doubt, and controlled by the habits of your life of sin. Your promises and resolutions are like ropes of sand. You cannot control your thoughts, your impulses, your affections. The knowledge of your broken promises and forfeited pledges weakens your confidence in your own sincerity and causes you to feel that God cannot accept you; but you need not despair. What you need to understand is the true force of the will. This is the governing power in man, the power of decision, or of choice. Everything depends on the right action of the will. The power of choice

God has given to men; it is theirs to exercise.
You cannot change your heart, you cannot of
yourself give to God its affections; but you can
choose to serve Him. You can give Him your
will; He will then work in you to will and to
do according to His good pleasure. Thus, your
whole nature will be brought under the control
of the Spirit of Christ; your affections will be
centered upon Him, your thoughts will be in
harmony with Him."

"Desires for goodness and holiness are
right as far as they go; but if you stop here,
they will avail nothing. Many will be lost while
hoping and desiring to be Christians. They do
not come to the point of yielding the will to
God. They do not choose to be Christians."

"Through the right exercise of the will,
an entire change may be made in your life. By
yielding up your will to Christ, you ally yourself
with the power that is above all principalities
and powers. You will have strength from
above to hold you steadfast, and thus through
constant surrender to God you will be enabled
to live the new life, even the life of faith." Steps
to Christ pages 46-48.

So, what is this saying? Simply this. We are
not able in and of ourselves to surrender all to
Jesus. It is impossible and goes against our human
nature. We can however choose to serve Him. If
we choose to serve Jesus, if this is our desire, we
can give that choice to serve Him and He will take

that choice and transform our will in conformity with His own. Once we have chosen to surrender to Christ, to obey Him, when we surrender that choice to Him, He will take that and give us the power to obey Him. Without His power we are trying to do it on our own and that is impossible. We must choose to allow Jesus to do for us what we really desire but do not have the power to accomplish. When we do this, He will supply the power. *"But as many as received Him, to them He gave the power to become sons and daughters of God, to everyone who believed on His name."* John 1:12. (KJV) We simply give Jesus our will or power of choice. He takes it and sanctifies it and gives it back to us, purified. We are born again not of the earthly but of the spiritual realm. Old things are died, all things are new.

A while back I shared a few excerpts from Frank Laubach's journal. Earlier I mentioned Brother Lawrence, the 16th century monk who may have been the first to implement the practice of the presence of Jesus. I would like to share a few letters he sent to some of his associates.

Conversation with a Friend August 3, 1666. "God did me a glorious favor in bringing me to a conversion at the age of eighteen.

In winter, I saw a tree stripped of its leaves and I knew that within a little time the leaves would be renewed, and that afterwards the flowers and the fruit would appear. From this I received a high view of the power and providence of God which has never since departed from my soul. The view I grasped that day set me completely loose from the world and kindled in me such a love for God that I cannot tell whether it has increased during the more than forty years since that time.

I was a footman to M. Fieubert, the treasured, but I am a very awkward fellow and seemed to break everything.

I decided, instead of continuing as a footman, to be received into a monastery. I thought that perhaps there I would be made, in some way, to suffer for my awkwardness and for all the faults I had committed. I decided to sacrifice my life with all its pleasures to God. But He greatly disappointed me in this idea, for I have met with nothing but satisfaction in giving my life over to Him.

I have found that we can establish ourselves in a sense of the presence of God by continually talking with Him. It is simply a shameful thing to quite conversing with Him to think of trifles and foolish things. We should feed and nourish our souls with high notions of God which will yield great joy. . .

The Most Excellent Method. Let me just comment with an open heart about my manner of going to God. All things hinge upon your hearty renunciation of everything which you are aware does not lead to God. You need to accustom yourself to continual conversation with Him – a conversation which is free and simple. We need to recognize that God is always intimately present with us and address Him every moment. In things that are doubtful, we need to ask His assistance to know His will. And the things we plainly see He requires of us; we should rightly perform. As we go about this pursuit, we should simply offer all things to Him before we do them and give Him thanks when we have finished.

In your conversation with God, be also employed in praising Him, adoring Him, and loving Him incessantly, doing all these things because of His infinite goodness and His perfection…

The most excellent method I have found of going to God is that of doing common business without any view to pleasing men, and as far as I am capable, doing it purely for the love of God.

It is a great delusion to think that the time of prayer ought to be different from other times. We are strictly obligated to adhere to God in the time of action, just as we are to adhere to prayer during the season of prayer.

My prayers are nothing other than a sense of the presence of God. My soul is simply insensible, at that time to anything but divine love. When the appointed time of prayer has passed, I find no difference because I continue with God, praising and blessing Him with all my might, so that I might pass my life in continual joy.

Consecration. . . If a Christian is to truly practice the presence of his Lord, and do so properly, then the heart of that Christian must be empty of all else. All. Why? Because God wills to possess that heart, and He wills to be the only possessor of that heart, and the only possession in that heart. He cannot be the only possessor of your heart unless it is empty of all else. He cannot put what He desires into a heart unless that heart has been left vacant for Him alone to refill it.

Do you know the highest kind of life we can experience? There is no other life in all the world as sweet and as delightful as the life lived in a continual walk with God. Even as I write such a statement, I realize that the only ones who can comprehend it are those who have practiced and experienced that unbroken walk with the Lord.

Let me quickly add that I do not advise you to walk this way simply because it is 'sweet and delightful!' it is not pleasure which we seek. Let this exercise be done from one motive alone, because we love Him. We walk with Him because it is His desire and His purpose that we walk with Him.

If I were a preacher, above everything else I would preach the practice of dwelling in the presence of Christ. If I had its ear, I would advise all the world to practice His presence; this is how necessary and how easy I think it to be.

Oh! If we but knew the need we have of God's presence. If we could only see how greatly we need the Lord's assistance in everything. If we could really see how helpless we are without Him, we would never lose sight of Him. Not even for a moment."

So now you have heard from Brother Lawrence. He walked with his Lord for forty some years. He made it a practice to be in a constant state of surrender to Jesus. I have shared these things with you so you can have input as to how you can start and maintain your own relationship with Jesus. Each one of us must work out our own relationship with Jesus. We are all different. Jesus relates to each one in a different way. For some, one way works better than another. The important thing is that we make developing a personal relationship with Jesus the priority in our life. We must put Him first in all we do. Though we do not have the power to surrender to Him we can choose to surrender and give that choice to Him. He will then take that choice and make it His own. We can desire to follow Him, and He will take that desire and make it His own and our own because we are in Him and He in us. So why would you want to do this? What reason do we have to make Jesus and a friendship with Him the number one priority in our life? Over these last few days together, we will explore the root reasons for following Jesus.

Matthew 6:33, 34

"But seek ye first the kingdom of God, and his righteousness; and all these things shall be added unto you. Take therefore no thought for the morrow: for the morrow shall take thought for the things of itself. Sufficient unto the day is the evil thereof."

Day Twenty-Five

A Sabbath to Remember

I chose to give this section a title. It is called "A Sabbath to Remember," because the time has come for you to put into practice for one complete day some of the concepts we have explored so far in this book. The best day to choose to give yourself totally, 100% to practicing the presence of Jesus is on a Sabbath Day. On this day you are not working. You can probably get away from your family if you really want to. I would like you to choose a Sabbath Day soon and seek out Jesus. On this special Sabbath, plan to really experience what it means to Worship God. I believe it is safe to say that not one in a thousand worship God on His day of rest in a way that it is their privilege to do so. In the next couple of days, I will outline a method of worshiping Jesus that few have experienced. Over the years I have given more than one Sabbath like this to Jesus and the rewards have been inspiring. I would like to say that every Sabbath with Jesus is this way for me, but I cannot. Time and time again I have come up to the Sabbath and experienced only a shadow of what could have been. I have slept away thousands of precious hours that could have been spent in communion with my re-Creator and my God. I have missed countless blessing from the gates of heaven. Oh, but when the floodgates have been opened, when He has come to spend the day with me and I with Him, it has been wonderful indeed.

When does the Sabbath start? According to Genesis, the evening and the morning were the first, second, third, fourth, fifth, sixth and seventh day. This would indicate that the Sabbath starts Friday at sundown. In planning your special Sabbath with Jesus, you might as well start this day on Friday evening at sundown. The Sabbath pre-dates sin. It was an institution established before Adam and Eve partook of the forbidden fruit. Genesis tells us that the world was created in six days and on the seventh day God rested. *"Thus, the heavens and the earth, and all the host of them, were finished. And on the seventh day God ended His work which He had done, and He rested on the seventh day. Then God blessed the seventh day and sanctified it, because in it He rested from all His work which God had created and made."* Genesis 2:1-3. (KJV) From the beginning of this world, Jesus has set aside this special time to meet with each of His children. He has never missed a Sabbath with them. They have often missed meeting with Him during this special time, but He has always been there for them.

In Isaiah 66:22-23, (KJV) we find out this is the way it will be for eternity. Jesus will have a special day of worship every Sabbath, forever

"And it shall come to pass, that from one new moon to another and from one Sabbath to another shall all flesh come to worship before me, saith the Lord." If we are going to spend every Sabbath day for eternity worshiping Jesus, and Jesus set aside this special time and sanctified it, why not put that into practice here and now so we will be right at home with Him in heaven and in the earth made new?

What should you do on your special Sabbath with Jesus? I would suggest that you plan to vacate your family for this one day. I would also suggest that you vacate your church for this day. Our enemy has ways to disrupt our best intentions. If he can use a family member or some incident at church to direct you away from worship of your Creator, he will do so. If he feels your affections being drawn off toward God, he will not easily relinquish up his control over you. He will use every means at his disposal to keep you from this time with Jesus. If people he has controlled for years and years suddenly turn their complete attention to the worship of God, do you think he is going to set back and do nothing? On this special Sabbath, plan it far enough in advance to enable you to come to Jesus alone. If you have been reading this book with a spouse, perhaps they can go with you to your special place and have their own time alone with Jesus. I must urge the importance of coming to Jesus alone though. Throughout the scriptures we see examples of the great men of faith spending time alone with Jesus.

Enoch is the first ancient that comes to mind who spent hours alone with Jesus. He would go into a place of quiet retreat and fill up his soul with the Bread of Heaven. He would drink from the fountains of Living Water that flowed from the throne of God. Then coming back from these quiet retreats, he would minister to the needs of his brothers and sisters. Noah, Abraham, Job, Jacob, Moses, Daniel, Paul, and countless other Bible greats took the time to meet with their Creator and their God, alone.

There is also the example of Jesus. From His earliest years, He took this time to communicate with His Father in Heaven, alone. From those places of quiet retreat, He came back to the multitudes filled with the Spirit of God. Nothing was impossible for Him. He could walk on water and still the stormy sea. He could bid the lame to walk and the blind to see. If Jesus, who was born with a sinless nature felt the need to go to a quiet place and pray how much more should we who are born of the flesh, with natures that are not in harmony with God, choose to spend as much time alone with Him as possible. How else are we going to find out where He wants us to go, find out what He wants us to be and know how to do what He wants us to do–go, be, do. So, go to the calendar now and pick your special Sabbath.

I would also like to suggest that on this special Sabbath you try to get out into nature. This is quite easy for most of us nine months out of the year when the weather is tolerable.

With proper attire a portion of this Sabbath can be spent with Jesus out in nature during the winter but the need for warmth will often make it necessary to spend a portion of this Sabbath within. The gates of heaven can still open to you within. Nature is best though. From the pages of its books the love of God can be read in the flower, the tiny insect, the animal that makes its home among the meadows or the woods. The songs of the birds can help you in lifting your own voice up in praise to your Creator. On this Sabbath, choose a place of quiet retreat in nature. Jesus favored this environment to all others. Even when in Jerusalem, He often choose the Mount of Olives for a retreat with his disciples.

Some who are accustomed to fasting might choose to leave food behind during this special time. Have you ever fasted for a day? If you have not, then it would probably be best on this special Sabbath to take along some food. Even if your mind were clearer without it the cry of your body for nourishment might interfere with your talk with God. Even while eating, you can make the entire time an act of worship to your Creator. If you decide to take food along though make it as natural as possible. Fresh or dried fruit, a few nuts or grains can go a long way to curb your need for food. Raw vegetables can also be used. It really would not hurt for you to share a sandwich or two with Jesus either. After all, when He fed the 5000 men plus women and children. He multiplied five loaves of bread and two fish into twelve baskets of food remaining after all were filled.

What else will you need to take with you? A Bible is entirely essential. What would a retreat with Jesus be without the Living Word? The Bible was written for our admonishment and instruction. From its pages, the Word of Life has been passed from generation to generation. The same Creator who spoke worlds into existence can speak to your soul from its sacred pages. A portion of your special Sabbath could be spent in committing to memory passages of Scripture. *"Thy Word have I hid in mine heart that I might not sin against thee."* Psalms 119:11. (KJV) I have found that during these special times with Jesus, passages of Scripture have been the catalyst to great conversations between me and my Lord. Bible passages that failed to inspire me have been transformed through the divine inspiration of Jesus when shared with Him alone. There have been brought to the surface of my mind meaningful answers to troubling questions that have plagued my soul. When the Word of God is studied in the presence of the Word of Life, infinite possibilities are opened to the diligent seeker of truth. So, take your Bible or a couple of different versions with you when you go to meet with Jesus.

I have found that a hymn book is also nice to take along to this place of quiet retreat with Jesus. Melody has a way of putting into our mind's messages of truth. If the birds can sing why can't we? If it is important for them to praise their Creator in this manner so can we. Earlier in this book I spoke about sharing music with Jesus.

There is a rich source of inspirational reading within the pages of the Spirit of Prophecy. Ellen White spent thousands of hours in the presence of Jesus. From her pen the Word has come alive and is there waiting for your enjoyment. Take some of her books with you if you like. When you share some of these things with Jesus, even greater meaning can be drawn from the Word of God. As Jesus revealed things to her so you can enter her experiences with Him. She, above all the great writers in history, had the privilege of walking on streets of gold in the presence of her Lord in the world to come. She was an eyewitness to hundreds of Bible stories. Through visions God granted her special insights into the mystery of holiness.

Another couple of items that you can take with you on your trip to the heart of God is a notebook and pen. As your Creator opens new insights to you, write them down so you can review them later. It is easy to forget the words of Jesus. As you write though, you can maintain the open lines of communication. Since the age of computer, the pen or pencil have been used a lot less. Your handwriting may have suffered. As I write in my own journal on these special times, I might say something like this to Jesus.

"Jesus?"

"Yes, Donielle."

"I am writing some of these thoughts down as you bring them to my attention. I would like to be able to go back and read this later but my handwriting after a while tends to get a little less legible. Help me to write neatly so I can come back and relive these precious moments with you again later."

"I will, Donielle."

"Thank you, Jesus."

"You are welcome, Donielle." Jesus in talking with you will often call you by name. When He talks with me, He sometimes calls me by name. Remember a few weeks ago we quoted that Bible text from Isaiah. "I have called you by name for you are mine." Sometimes He calls me, "Son." Sometimes I hear Him whisper, "Friend." It is very comforting to be called "Friend". Abraham was called "The Friend of God."

There are some things you should not take along with you on this special Sabbath with Jesus. You may have been thinking this Sabbath in nature would give you time to find that special photo to send to a friend or print on a calendar.

You might also think this would be a great time to gather some video footage of what you see in the wilderness or woods. I would like to remind you though; you are not going out in nature to take pictures or get that one in a million photograph. You are going there to meet with your Creator and your God. You are going there to worship Him. A cell phone might be okay to take with you in case of an emergency, but it should be shut off. A family member or friend will surely find a reason to call you if they can get through. Thus, your mind will be drawn away from your purpose in meeting with God. I would not recommend taking any cassette players, radios, or portable CD players to play your favorite spiritual songs. As good as this may seem, these devices will drown out the voice of God speaking to your soul. In the world today life is fast paced. This generation has been brought up to be entertained. On this special Sabbath though you do not need to be entertained. You need to seek the face of Jesus and let Him give you some necessary instructions to guide you on your journey toward eternal life.

In today's chapter, we have outlined some of the things you should consider in planning your special Sabbath with Jesus. In summary plan to spend this entire day alone with Jesus away from the influence of family and friends. Your Sabbath will start Friday evening at sundown. You will go to a place of quiet retreat, preferable in nature away from the hustle and bustle. In this place away from unnatural sounds, the voice of

God can be more readily discerned. Plan to take a Bible, perhaps a hymn book and possibly some of the writings of Ellen White or some other inspiration author. A little food is okay and when shared with Jesus can be used to give glory to your Creator. You might like to take a notebook with you to write down some of the meaningful experiences you have with Jesus. Leave behind modern inventions like digital cameras, cell phones, portable music players or other toys that could distract from your quality time with Jesus. Finally, during this special time, you will enter true worship. Your goal is to find out what it truly means to worship God with your heart, mind, and soul. Tomorrow I will outline how to approach this special Sabbath in more detail.

"In the past God spoke to our forefathers through the prophets at many times and in various ways, but in these last days he has spoken to us by his Son, whom he appointed heir of all things, and through whom he made the universe. The Son is the radiance of God's glory and the exact representation of his being."

Hebrews 1:1-3

Day Twenty-Six

Perhaps this happens to be the day you plan to take time with Jesus. Let us assume it is close to sundown on Friday. As the precious hours of this special Sabbath have drawn near, you have a note of expectancy in your being. The time has nearly come for you to enter rest with your Creator. Perhaps on this special Friday, you left your place of employment earlier than usual. Upon arriving at your home, you packed those things you plan to take with you. If you are taking a backpack trip into the wilderness, you have it filled with clothes, food, Bibles, fire starting equipment, sleeping bag, tent, etc. Your shower has been taken and you have put on a fresh change of clothes. All your work has ended. You get in your vehicle and head for the hills. It would be nice to arrive there before the Sabbath hours begin. Perhaps several hours if you plan to hike into the mountains and set up camp somewhere. It would be nice as sundown approaches to be in your place of quiet retreat with your tent all set up, ready to meet with your Friend, Jesus.

What now? How should you begin? To start with, we need to enter a state of holiness. We need to be covered with the righteousness of Jesus Christ. Our sins need to be confessed and covered by the blood of the Lamb. If we are to understand the spiritual issues Jesus wants for us, we must be in a spiritual state of mind, for spiritual things are spiritually discerned. On the next few pages, you will enter a conversation I might have with Jesus on a Special Sabbath with Him. Since I did not have the computer to write everything down on my backpack weekend, some of this happened, some did not. This may or may not be the type of communication you have established with Jesus at this time. We are all different, but we all understand conversational prayer with Jesus. This type of prayer is simply talking to Jesus as you would a friend and allowing Him to either speak to you or direct the thoughts of your own mind into a form of conversation between the two of you. If you are covered by the righteousness of Christ, your thoughts and conversation with Him will reflect it.

I reached my place of quiet retreat. The Sabbath hours came quickly. I chose a place in the mountains. It is called Merritt Lake. It truly is a backpacker's paradise. I had to put on a generous portion of bug repellant. The mosquitoes would have loved to ensure the survival of their species with the aid of my blood had I not protected myself. I set up my tent. The hike was a bit difficult. My backpack weighed in at around 45 pounds. I hiked 2.75 miles up a steep path that gained over 2000 feet in elevation. In Central Washington there are hundreds of get-a-way places like this where in the solitude of the mountains one can find a place to be alone with God.

As the precious hours of the Sabbath draw near a sense of my great need of Jesus came over me. I had been setting on a collapsible camp stool by the fire. But I felt the need to fall on my face. There were some things in my life that had come between my soul and my Savior. So, entering my tent I lay face down on my sleeping bag and for the next several moments turned my soul over to the searching eyes of my Creator. In my mind I was lifted toward heaven. I was being baptized in the light of His glory. As I entered His presence, all within me that was not in harmony with His Kingdom of Heaven, stood out as dark and barren. There in the presence of Jesus I allowed the Physician to examine me. Nothing was hidden from His eye. After a few moments with Him there, surrender came. I gave all those dark areas to Him.

"Lord, Here I am. Take me. Take away these things that are separating me from You. All of them. Come into my heart and abide with me." Then resting in His love, I allowed Him to do His work. Sometimes He points out specific areas of my life I am holding unto. We struggle for a while; He gently tries to remove them while I am still trying to cling to them. This type of communication is often wordless. It is a giving and receiving. Sometimes I do not even know what unharmonious part of my life I am surrendering to Jesus. I do not need to know. The mere mention of this unholy area by Jesus could start a whole series of dark thoughts that would draw me away from the relationship I hope to attain with Him. There lying face down in homage to God, the moment finally came when we were one. Everything had been given to Jesus.

At this point, meaningful communication between my Lord and I often begins. Sometimes though there is silence. I try to start a conversation with Him, but I hear no responding voice. In these instances, I continue to rest in the presence of Jesus and search my soul to see if there is anything, I am still holding onto that would prevent His full presence.

"Help me, Lord. I long for some word from You. I am here, Jesus. I have come to this place of retreat to meet with You. It is Your Sabbath day. You have set this time apart, sanctified it, made it holy. It is a time when You make Yourself available to meet with me. I am here, waiting, Jesus. Come." At this time, a burden for some friends in trouble came powerfully to my thoughts. On the way up to this quiet retreat, I would often rest and lift them up to the Lord in Prayer. Now an urgency came to do it again. As I was talking with the Lord about these people, He shared with me that another one of their children would die. About four years had passed since they lost a 16-year-old son in an automobile accident. When I heard the news about another child being torn from them, I had such anguish I cannot describe. I fell back down to the sleeping bag and while digging my fingers into its folds asked the Lord.

"Why must they suffer more, Lord? haven't they gone through enough?". I wept for them. What would become of them? Would they survive? The loss of their first son about killed them. The Lord assured me His grace was sufficient for them.

NOTE: (While reviewing this writing I am adding this note. My friends did lose another child a few months later. It was another son. This one was 13 when his brother was killed. His name was Joshua. He was 17 at the time of his death. I tell you this not to prove what I am writing to be true, but to share with you that the Lord needed me to know ahead of time what would happen so I could be an agent of the Holy Spirit to help prepare them and support them in this new crisis. Their faith in God was severely shaken. The pain was so great, they separated for a time, but God in His mercy brought them back together and has now given them three grandchildren to fill those two empty places in their hearts. When I shared with them the foreknowledge God had shared with me, the faith of the father was strengthened a little. He was beginning to doubt what he believed to be true about God. He even tried on his own life but was found in time by his daughter. As of the second publishing of this book, both he and his wife are strong in their faith in God. May He be praised glorified and uplifted)

I was rather tired after the hike up the steep trail and emotionally drained from entering that intercessory secession of prayer with my Lord. I was also very hungry. On this trip I decided not to fast. A portion of the weight in my pack was food. Moving out of my tent I added wood to the fire and set about making something to eat. I wanted a good meal. At the pump I collected some water and opened a packet of instant mashed potatoes. Soon they were all fluffy and nice. I grilled some protein over the fire on a telescoping grilling stick, pulled out some bread. Between the sandwich and potatoes, I was feeling much better by the time they were consumed. After the meal, I heard a word from above.

"The sun is passing behind the mountains, Donielle. Come out and enjoy it with Me. Look at the clouds. See the colors? Open your ears. Do you hear that bird singing its evening song? I created it for your enjoyment. Over there, listen, Son. Do you hear that mountain robin? Something is coming too close to its nest. Do you hear the note of alarm in its call? Someday, Donielle, this world of sin will pass. The robin will no longer fear for her young. The curse will be lifted. Walk with Me, will you?"

"Yes, Lord. Where do You want to go?"

"This way, Friend. Come down near the lake. I want to show you some things." As I approached the lake it was colored pink from the reflections of the clouds. A slight breeze was blowing, and I saw the rippled effect in the water. Above the

lake, the mountains stood unmoving yet in the lake the reflections were placid. They moved back and forth with the ripples. I sensed Jesus nearby. I lean slightly in His direction and sensed Him pointing to the ripples.

"Do you see the reflection of the mountain, Donielle?"

"Yes, Jesus. It is moving back and forth with the ripples."

"Much of life here in this world of sin is like that. There is nothing secure. You may feel secure in your home or place of work, but it can be gone in a moment. The day is coming when it will all die. You have a lot of things you have collected over the years, Donielle. You hold on to them thinking that someday you will need them. There is quite a bit of clutter around your home. Work with me, Son. Together we can bring more order to your life. Those things you are holding unto will die one day. They are like the ripples. Hold on to the true and the sure. Hold on to what will last for eternity. For now, the mountains above this lake are unmoved. A day will come when they will move though. When I return for My own, every mountain and island will be moved out of their places, but for now, they are unmoving. I want to help form a character in you that is unmoving, Donielle. This character will stand true and sure on that day when I move these mountains.

"Do you really want me to be with You, Jesus?"

"*Yes, Son. I want you to be with Me, to return with Me to heaven when I come for you. I prepared a special place for you in a city that will never die. I want to spend eternity with you. From that city we will often travel to wonders you can never imagine this side of heaven. I love you, Donielle. Do you love, Me?*"

"You know all things, Jesus. When you look into my heart do you see that I have love for you?"

"*Sometimes, Donielle. Sometimes I see that love and I can feel it but there are many times when I sense you do not wish to have Me around. Why, Donielle? Why do you want to live apart from Me so much of the time? Can't you see when I am with you and you are with Me, life is sweeter, dearer, more wonderful and more peaceful?*"

"Yes, Jesus. When I am with You like this, I feel complete. You are in me and I am in You. I am at peace with myself and my brothers and sisters. When I am with You like this, Jesus, the love You have for me reaches out through me and I love others. I see them with Your eyes."

"*Don't you think it would be best, Donielle to be this way all the time? If you allowed Me to be in you always and you always in Me, I could use you to minister to these who I love so dearly. They do not know what it means to abide in Me. They do not understand that each breath is a drawing in of the divine nature and an exhaling of the sinful one. They do not know that each moment they are filled with My presence the enemy cannot possess them. What I need from My people today is to have them understand the true nature of abiding in Me. They not only need to understand it but experience it. I have My children all over the world. They have the potential of doing a great work. If they would abide in Me, moment by moment, hear My guiding voice in their life and obey it, we could prepare the world for My return. When I come in the clouds of heaven, there would be people all over the world who would be waiting and looking for Me."*

For a while there was silence between Jesus and me. We were on the shores of the small lake. I looked in the water and there in the fading light saw a tiny minnow. A thought springs to my mind. I have a question for Jesus. What can I learn from that minnow?

"A fish has to stay in water, Donielle or it will die. Just as you require air to breath, so the fish requires water. The Son of Man came to give life and give it more abundantly. This minnow will spend its life in this small lake unaware of the massive world that surrounds it. Man, likewise, if he does not come to experience what it means to abide in Me, is destined to spend his entire life in this world, unaware of the more abundant life I long for him to experience in the earth made new."

"Could you take Me back to your world with you, Donielle?"

"I suppose I could, Jesus. If I wanted to."

"Why wouldn't you want to?"

"I don't know, Lord. When I am with You it is wonderful. I have taken You with me on a number of occasions, haven't I, Jesus?"

"Yes, you have, but the times when I have not been an active part of your life far outweigh those times when I have. Why are you so reluctant to become converted?"

"I suppose it is about time, Jesus. In my work there is always something to do. I am a creature of habit. I get up and do each day what I have done for years. I dress, eat sometimes, and head off to work. I put myself to the task of doing what needs to be done."

"Is your work of lasting value, Don, I can call you Don, can't I?"

"Yes, Jesus. You can call me Don. If you mean will my work die, yes Jesus. It is not of lasting value. The people I work for though are Your children, Jesus. If they form a relationship with You, that can last for eternity. But what might that mean to me?"

"Why don't you help them do this, Don?"

"Do what, Jesus?"

"*Help them form a character they can take with them into eternity.*"

"I don't know how, Jesus. Many of them seem to be church people. They have their religious beliefs. When I talk with them about spiritual things, they assure me they are Christians also. How do I carry You to them? How do I help them understand who you are and that you long to open to them a new universe of spiritual life, one with infinite possibilities? If I shared with them how we can walk and talk together, Jesus, wouldn't they think me a bit crazy?"

"*Does it matter, Son?*"

"I suppose in the light of eternity, Jesus, it doesn't, but in the short run I am there to provide a service. I go in and do the work we have agreed on then move on to the next job. I have little opportunity to open up a spiritual conversation with them and still be productive."

"*Will your work last, Donielle?*"

"No, Jesus. You know it will not last. Eventually it will die but so long as the world is as it is, so long as the earth remains You, yourself have clearly stated there will be sunshine and rain, seedtime, and harvest. How am I to do more than that?"

"*If you were in communion with me moment by moment, Don, would you need to know more?*"

"No, I suppose not. If I were in communion with you moment by moment and You knew these people's spiritual needs, I expect You could tell me what You wanted me to do while I was in their service."

"*Could you do this, Donielle? Could you take Me with you to work?*"

"With You, Jesus. All things are possible."

"*Would you take Me with you to work next Monday, Son?*"

"Wow! Lord. You drive a hard bargain. Can I think about it for a while, Jesus?"

"*What is there to think about?*"

"Could we move onto something else, Jesus, to some other topic for a little bit. If not, Lord. If it is not your will for us to do this at this time then give me an example of what it would be like if I took you to work with me and we were working on the K's project, Monday.

"*I have already opened the door for you to talk with Mrs. K. Do you remember when you took her around to the various nurseries to pick out the types of plants she liked?*"

"Yes, Jesus. We spent 3 hours on Friday doing that."

"*Do you remember how a week from this coming Wednesday she wants you to come to the creative writing class she is teaching and share your experience with publishing your book, 'A Little Taste of Heaven?'*"

"Yes, Jesus."

"*Do you remember discussing Christian education with her in the home schooling of her daughters and comparing that to the public-school system?*"

"Yes."

"*She is one of My children, Don. I have plans to spend eternity with her. She shared with you her specialty in English. You lack a lot in that area, Donielle.*"

"I am aware of that, Jesus. English is something I have a clumsy grasp on, especially when it comes to using proper format for sentences."

"*She offered her services to you, Don. Please take Me with you when you landscape their home. I want her and her family to understand more of the abundant life I came to this world to give men and woman like the K's. Let her do the work she agreed to do for you. The information you have compiled speaks of that more abundant life this precious family can experience.*"

"Thank you, Jesus for this example. Over the next few days, I am landscaping their home and in whatever future encounters You might design for me and this family, have Thine own way, Lord. Have Thine own way. Our enemy will try to see that I forget this conversation we have had here. Will you remind me, Jesus to take you with me to work when I do their place?"

"*Yes, Don I will.*"

"Jesus."

"*Yes, Don.*"

"Over the last few years, you have brought me into contact with Mr. B. When I look at him, I see little hope of him ever coming to a knowledge of you. Do you have a plan for his life?"

"*Yes, I do.*"

"Do you have a work for me to do in his behalf?"

"*Yes.*"

"What is it Jesus?"

"*For now, Donielle, you need to let him know that you know Me. He needs to see you as one who is acquainted with the Creator of the heavens and the earth. He needs to see Me in you. If you take Me with you in your personal contact with him, I can see he understands that you can be trusted to speak with him about his soul needs. Become his friend but more than, that let him know that you have a knowledge of spiritual things. If you do this or allow Me to do this through you, a time may come when*" *he will ask you a spiritual question about something that is troubling him. Be sure I am with you if he asks that question."*

"I sensed a bit of doubt, Jesus. There was that if? Will it sadden You IF that opportunity never comes?"

"Donielle, take Me be sure I am in you and you in Me whenever you meet with him, then leave the results of his response to Me."

"So, it all comes back to the same thing, Jesus. I need to remain in You. I need to be sure You are my personal companion and guide all the time whether in this place of quiet rest or on the job.

It was late by this time and the sun had set. As I looked back toward my tent, I could see the fire had died down. I wondered if I should place some more wood on it and stay up for a while longer or slip off to sleep? I finally decided to do the latter. On the way up the mountain, I had worked up quite a sweat. My shirt had been soaked through. As I felt it now on the branch not far from the fire, it was nearly dry. By morning it would be unless a heavy dew came. I decided to leave it there hanging on the branch not far from my tent. What I did not realize was that I had pitched my tent nearly on top of a game trail. Deer and other woodland animals often took this rout down to drink from the lake. Perhaps on this night the scent of that shirt acted as a deterrent causing them to select an alternate route?

*"And they shall dwell safely in the wilderness,
and sleep in the woods. And I will make them,
and the places found about my hill a blessing.*
Ezekiel 34:25, 26

Day Twenty-Seven

How was your evening? Did you rest well? If you are reading this chapter in your place of quiet retreat with Jesus, then today should be the Sabbath. The chances of this though are less than one in seven. And if you brought this book along with you to read, you should not have. This special Sabbath is for you and Jesus to enjoy together. Did you allow Jesus to wake you up this morning? If you did, what time was it? Jesus never slumbers and never sleeps. In Psalm 121:3, 4 we read

"He will not suffer thy foot to be moved: he that keepeth thee will not slumber. Behold, he that keepeth Israel shall neither slumber nor sleep." (KJV) **If** you slept in the woods last evening you probably did not get as much rest as you would at home in your own bed. The night was filled with new sounds and a sleeping bag or camper bed is not as comfortable as the one in your own bedroom, but never-the-less the fresh air did you good. This morning your mind should be clear.

I was awakened early. I do not know exactly at what time because I did not want to take my watch. During the week I am directed by that watch. It dictates what time I must get up, get ready and go to work, when and where I will go and what I must get done. I did not want that pressure this Sabbath. While still laying down I directed my thoughts to Jesus. All night long He had been with me waiting for the dawn of consciousness. Would I remember Jesus when I woke up? Jesus wanted to be sure I did.

"*Good morning, Donielle. How are you today?*" I rubbed my eyes a little and tried to regain a conscious state of mind. Outside it was still dark but the air was already filled with the sounds of the woodland birds. They must have known their Creator was in the woods with them this Sabbath morning because they were especially happy. I could hear it in their singing. Then the voice of Jesus registered in my mind.

"Good morning, Jesus." I said it out loud. Today on this special Sabbath I decided to talk out loud to Jesus. When we speak to Him in thought only, there are more distractions. Our thinking process functions much faster than we can keep up with. While we are trying to listen to the voice of our Creator, ten other thoughts are vying for our attention. Why not talk to Jesus out loud then? There was no one around to listen and think I am crazy. After saying "Good morning, I waited for Jesus to speak next. I wanted Him to lead out in this Sabbath rest rather than myself.

Some tents are very damp in the morning. All night long your breath has been going up. Without proper ventilation, this can condense on the top and side of your tent. The designers of this tent were good. I decided to set up and lean back against the side. I pictured Jesus there with me. He had His arm around me, and I leaned back on His chest. For several moments I cherished this closeness. There is nothing like His love anywhere. His love is so consuming, so comforting. The words of an old hymn came to mind. "Safe in the arms of Jesus, safe on His gentle breast. Here by His love o'er shaded. Sweetly my soul doth rest." And so, it was. As I rested there in His arms it was wonderful indeed. Finally, He spoke.

"*When the Father, the Holy Spirit and I were in conference, way before this earth was created, We decided I was to be the Creator of a new order of beings. We laid our plans carefully. As Creator, I was to be sovereign ruler of this world even as I was ruler over the rest of the universe. The Three of us are of one mind. In a matter of what would be earthly seconds, several possibilities passed between us. We would create independent beings with the capacity to love, think, fellowship with Us, and can procreate, to multiply and fill the whole earth. This new order of being would be the caretakers of their own world even as I was the caretaker of the universe. We envisioned a planet filled with happy people who would give praise and homage to their Creator. With the plan, we also saw the problem that would arise. We knew the results would not turn out like the perfect picture we envisioned, at least not for planet earth. First though, We saw the world, perfect as it came forth from My hand. It was a beautiful picture, Don. Adam and Eve were in that picture. They were happy and filled with deep love for Me. Our companionship was wonderful. I walked and talked with them just as I am talking with you. They had the advantage of fellowship with Me in the physical realm, though. I was present with them in body. They could touch Me and see Me. We could go to a fruit tree, gather its bounty, and share a meal together.*

When the Three of us, however, saw the results of this venture and all the misery and woe that would come because of sin, we came awfully close to abandoning this project. The Father's nature demands perfect obedience. It is the only way the universe can exist. There must be only one Lord, One God, One Ruler over all. At the same time though, since Our Kingdom is a Kingdom of love, it is essential that each member that makes up that universe choose to obey us out of love. When we saw that Adam and Eve would make the wrong choices, Our heart of love was broken. Had we abandoned the Creation Project, the loss of Adam and Eve would have broken our hearts. You see, Donielle, once they came into existence in our mind, you might say, they were already created, and we loved them. With the wrong choices they would make, it was essential for us to explore several different plans of Salvation for them. Several passed through Our mind but only one would meet the requirements of Our order of government. The only plan that would work would be for Me, their Creator, to become their perfect obedience. That would require that I come down and be one of them, born of man into a world of sin, a world that was in open rebellion toward its Creator. Had there been only earth to consider, perhaps we would have abandoned the Creation project. Earth is not the only planet with free willed beings. There are millions out there. But this world, this creation would be different. There were empty places in heaven vacated by Lucifer and his followers. These would one day be filled, replaced with the seed of Adam and Eve, two beings created in the very image of God. This order of being would have the physical trait of the Godhead represented by Myself. They would have the mental portion of the Godhead as represented by My Father and the Spiritual characteristic found in the third person of the Godhead, the Holy Spirit. Yes, humanity would be a special race of beings, a new order created in our very own image, designed for eternal fellowship with us for ages without end. Come with Me, Donielle. It is still dark out. We can still see a few bright stars."

I arose and left the tent with my friend. The heavy dew I had thought about before retiring, had fallen, and all nature was damp. We walked to a small clearing and peered up at the heavens. The eastern sky was starting to brighten but off to the west it was still dark enough to see a few stars. I spoke.

"You mentioned there are other inhabited planets in our own galaxy, Jesus."

"*Yes,*" was the reply.

"How far away is heaven?"

"Not as far as you might think, Don."

"How can that be, Jesus. They tell us it would take years traveling at the speed of light to reach the nearest star."

"Distance on earth is measured in a much different way than in the reality of the Kingdom of Heaven. Heaven is located quite close to earth. It is closer to earth than most of the other inhabited planets. The experience of sin had to be confined to this sun, this solar system. When My time came to become a man, the Father wanted to be close to Me. The New Jerusalem is mobile. It can travel through space. It traveled close to earth after the fall of Adam and Eve. We wanted to be near enough to them to keep watch yet far enough away to prevent sin from coming to Us. When the redeemed of the earth are gathered within, the Holy City will take a trip around the universe. I need witnesses, Donielle. I need people like you who were born in sin yet overcame by My blood to testify to the unfallen worlds on that trip. That is the future I have planned for My people. Before that happens though, I need people who will show the world what a person born of the Spirit is like. There are millions of people who are called by My name who do not know Me as it is their privilege to know Me. The Christian experience they have given their life in service for is only a shadow of what I would like it to be. They could have the privilege of My personal companionship moment by moment. They would

then experience a freedom like only a few have known." Jesus paused a moment in His discourse. Then continued.

"My people experience so little and suffer so much. I would love to ease their burdens to lighten their load. I would share in their sorrows and sooth their pain. How often I would have gathered them to Me, but they would not. They choose to go alone, to fight a battle with an enemy I have already conquered. Why don't they come to Me, Don? Why do each choose to go their own way? I would lead them all together into the Kingdom, but they will not follow Me, they won't even listen to My voice."

My thoughts were on the question Jesus had ask. "Why do the people called by Christ's name choose to go their own way?" I was one of those people. Most of my life had been that way. Day after day I went about my business as if there were no Creator God by my side ready to help. When troubles came, I bore them alone. Whether success or failure, Jesus was typically up there doing whatever it was He does up there and I was down here or so I thought. "Low I am with you always, Donielle even unto the end of the world."

The sun would soon rise. I felt the urge to walk to the top of a small hill overlooking the lake. It was chilly this morning. I had donned a jacket with a hood. At the top of the hill, I sat on a fallen log. A chipmunk chattered not far away scolding and giving warning to the other woodland creatures that I was there. Suddenly I felt a desperate need to cry out to Jesus, to ask Him some questions that were troubling me. Not far from the log, a small patch of grass grew. It was to this spot I fell and cried out to my friend beside me.

"Jesus, I have failed you so often. I have gone my own way, time and time again. I have lived my life as if I had no one to be accountable to. How stupid of me, Jesus. You have been there all the time waiting patiently for me. You have called and called, and I did not come. Why do you still seek me? I am not worthy to have you as a friend. I should not even be alive. I have sinned so many sins. The wages of sin are deaths, Jesus and that is what I deserve. Why me, Jesus? Why did you choose to keep chasing me after all the times I run away from you? Please forgive Lord, please forgive me. I do not know if I can be the witness You expect me to be. My nature is to do my own thing. To be one with You always, would require an entire change in my style of living. It would not be easy. A thousand things would have to change. Sometimes I do not want to change, Jesus. I like things the way they are most of the time. Tell me it would not be so bad, so hard as I think. Please, Jesus. I am crying out to You because You have called, and I do not want to answer. You have shown me where You want me to go but I do not want to go there. You have given me a picture of what You want me to be, but I do not want to be it. Is there any hope for me, Jesus? How can I do these things? I am afraid to give my life over to Your total control, to make You Lord of my life. Look at all the sacrifices I would be called to make. Jesus my sinful nature is struggling to hold me captive. Can you help? Will you help me, Jesus? This is a fearful thing You ask of me."

I was crying now. The whole future of my life seemed so hopeless. What would it be like to be under the command of Jesus? My love of the world would have to go. All the treasures I had accumulated, would I have to give them up? There were television programs I liked to watch. I had books in my library that should be burned. I began to realize what a hold the world had on me. I was not really a Christian though I believed in Christ at least not a born-again Christian. How could I be and still love the things of the world like I did? What Jesus was asking for was too hard. Where was He now, this Jesus, this person who called me friend? Then I sensed Him near me. His arm surrounded me. He overshadowed me and allowed His love to enter my wretched being.

"Give it all to Me, Donielle. Give it all to Me. All you must do is let go and trust Me. I am your Creator. I know what will make you happy. Your character, your talents, your nature is known to Me. There is a place where you can be all I want you to

be. I will open the doors. I will lead you there each step of the way. You do not have to think of all the things you will have to give up. I do not want you to dwell on all the mistakes you have made in the past. Forgetting what lies behind let us press on to the higher calling I have given you. But Don, please do not try to meet that calling alone. If you do, if you decide to get there in your own way, you will fail."

I lay on the damp grass along time. Looking back on this time now, I think Jesus wanted to share the sunrise with me that beautiful Sabbath morning, but I would not look up. Something in me wanted to hold on to what I had. After twenty minutes or so wallowing in self-pity, I got up and started walking aimlessly. How could I have done this after having the blessed assurance of the presence of Jesus just moments ago? I had set this time apart to worship my Creator yet even in this quiet, natural setting the enemy still had a hold on me. "Give them all, give them all. Give them all to Jesus. Shattered dreams, wounded hearts, and broken toys. Give them all, give them all, give them all to Jesus; and He will turn your sorrow into joy!"

After that song passed through my mind another one came. "The Savior is waiting to enter your heart, why don't you let Him come in? There is nothing in this world to keep you apart, what is your answer to Him? Time after time He has waited before and now, He is waiting again. To see if you are willing to open the door. Why, don't you let Him come in?" That was the question I had been pondering again. Why didn't I let Him come in? Hadn't Jesus said He would share though? I was in rebellion toward Him now. Would He share with me still? Would He help me with this struggle? In this state of mind did I even dare to ask His help? Why not try.

"Jesus, are you mad at me? Can I still talk to you even though I am struggling with this issue?"

"*Yes, Donielle, you can still talk to Me, and Don, I was never mad at you. Remember that text in the Bible that says 'Come let us reason together, saith the Lord. Though your sins be as scarlet they shall be as white as snow. Though they be red like crimson, they shall be as wool.*"

"Yes, Jesus. I remember that text."

"*Let us reason it out then, Don. Why would you want to hold on to your old life of sin and wretchedness? What does it have to offer you?*"

"Let us take one example, Jesus. The television series I like to watch. I see those characters going through all their needless pain and trouble and I want to tell them all the mistakes they are making. I keep hoping they will get smarter and figure out what is important in life, but they just keep getting deeper into trouble. I think in the end it will all work out though and I keep hoping for that to happen."

"*Your television program, Don. Is it something you can take with you to heaven?*"

"No."

"*Does it help to turn your thoughts toward Me?*"

"No, Jesus."

"*Is it helping you to be a better Christian, one with a mind that is controlled by the Holy Spirit?*"

"No."

"*So then in the light of eternity, what good is your television program?*"

"It has no heavenly good, Jesus. None."

"*Can you give it to Me then, Donielle?*"

"Yes, Jesus. I can give it to You. I do not need it in my life."

"*Was that so hard, Don?*"

"No, Jesus but what about next Thursday evening?"

"*Trust Me, Don. You do not need to watch that program. What else do you fear you will have to give up if you truly make Me Lord of your life?*"

"I have lots of toys, Jesus. I also have a little car. I really like it. It is fun to drive. It is small and especially during traffic it is easier to maneuver. It also gets good gas mileage. Will I have to give it up too?"

"*Do you need a car, Donielle?*"

"I think I do, Jesus. You know. Do I need a car?"

"*In today's society you do need a car, Don. You need one to do the work I want you to do over the next few months. You said it is easy on gas, it runs well, and you like to drive it. There is nothing wrong with that. You do not have to give up your car to serve Me, rather you can use it in service for Me.*"

"But what will people think when I drive up in it? Will they think of me as covetous?"

"*Does it really matter what people think of you, Donielle?*"

"I suppose it shouldn't. I remember a sentence in college that helped me deal with this in the past. It went something like this. 'We would think less about what people think of us if we realize they seldom do.'"

"*That has a lot of truth in it, Don. People are usually so caught up in their own life they do not think about others much. If they do, it usually does not last long. Do you remember those trips you took in the plane?*"

"Yes."

"*From the heavens you get a better picture of what I see when I look down on the earth. You saw postage stamp sized lots each with a miniature house and miniature cars and trucks. Each of those lots represents the life accumulations of some family. What they own is nothing. It can be gone in a moment. Yet millions will give up eternal life for those very possessions. The things of earth are fleeting, Don. They are perishable and will be gone one day.*"

211

What you have with Me though will last for eternity. Perhaps you should not look at all you will have to give up in coming to Me, rather look at what you will gain," Do you like the friendship I offer you?"

"Yes, Jesus."

"Are you at peace in My presence? Are you happy when you recognize that I am by your side?"

"Most of the time, Jesus it is fine. If I am not involved in some activity that is drawing me away from You, I really do appreciate Your companionship."

"Do you feel like you could spend eternity with Me, Donielle?"

"Yes, Jesus. I would love that."

"Are any of the things you are holding unto, things you feel are valuable enough to take with you to heaven?"

"Most of them are things I will not need in heaven, Jesus."

"Then do you really need them now?"

"Probably not as much as I think I need them. So, what should I do with my possessions?"   *"You can sell many of them or give them away. Take the money and invest it in souls that will go into our kingdom of heaven. Earlier in this book we focused on your need to get these things out of your life. A family can live simply within their means and have plenty to share with others. I will show you how so long as you keep Me first in your life."*

"Okay, Jesus. You are the Lord. You know what my future with You would be if I chose to surrender everything to You."

"So, what is holding you back now, Son?" Something about the way Jesus called me by that name got through to me.

"Just a few minutes ago, there were a thousand things I felt I would have to give up, to follow You completely. They don't seem all that important now though," I responded. Suddenly I wanted to give it all to Jesus, to trust in Him fully, to fully be His son, born again, born of His Spirit. In place of the father of lies and death I would trust in the Father of Truth and Life. There in that quiet place, away from the rapid pace I did give it all to Him. Jesus came in. I opened the door to Him, and we had sweet fellowship again. I knew that whatever the future held, whatever I might be called to give up would not be so bad. Jesus would replace it with something so much better I would never miss the old. I did not even have to give it all up at one time. I only had one moment at a time with Jesus. I could choose to give it all to Him this moment and the next and the next and the next. Truly He did know what was best.

The sun had risen. I had brought an apple with me along with my Bible. I thought of it now, tucked away in my pocket. I pulled it out.

"Tell me about this apple, Jesus. What can I learn from it?"

"*It is fruit from a tree.*"

"Yes. What else?"

"*It has a protective skin. The fruit you bear must also have a protective skin. This skin is not of self. The fruit you are called to bear for Me will not be fruit that will glorify you, Don. It will be fruit that will bring glory to Our Father in heaven. The fruit I call you to bear will not point to yourself but will point people to Me. To do this though you must be in Me and I in you. The fruit you are called to share will be of My Spirit.*"

"*If you are filled with My Spirit, the fruit you bear will be evidence of that. My spirit is represented by this protective skin. It protects the inner, sacred portion of the fruit from unholy influences. What would happen to this apple if you let it set out on your counter at home for several weeks?*"

"It would keep rather good, Jesus for a while. Eventually it would lose moisture and the skin would become wrinkled."

"*What would happen if you marred the skin of the apple before you let it set on your counter?*"

"Bacteria would enter the damaged area and the fruit would rot."

"*My Spirit is a protective shield. When you are surrounded with My righteousness you will produce fruit that brings glory to Me. Your sinful nature will not surface to mar the fruit and dishonor Me. Are you going to take a bite of this apple, Donielle?"*

"I don't think so, Jesus. Not now. I do not want to mar this fruit yet."

"But that is what some fruit is produced for, Don. It is grown to bring nourishment to the one who partakes of it. If the fruit is not spoiled, a blessing can be received from eating it. Your spiritual nature will be strengthened and in partaking of the blessing you will have a chance to praise Me."

"Okay, Jesus. I will just take a few moments to polish this apple, to be sure its skin is wiped clean of any impurities then we can share this apple together. Should I cut it with my knife or use the teeth you gave me?"

"I created you with a power of choice to make just such a decision, Don. You do not need to ask Me about that. In using your power of choice though, there are some issues dealing with spiritual matters that you can ask Me about. With those I will gladly help you to make the right choices."

As I look back on this experience, I realize there will be many times in the future when I will have to give it all to Jesus. This must be a daily practice. We need to do what has been called; "Pray through." To pray through we may often have to keep looking to the strength of Jesus through prayer or personal communion until we have come to that moment in time when we are willing to give it all to Jesus again. Paul called it "dying daily." Once we die to self, Jesus can come in and fully possess us. When we make a habit of this, we will find that it becomes easier each time, that our hold on the perishable things of earth is being broken as we look to Jesus.

Once I had surrendered my life to Jesus it was good to be there with Him in this place of quiet retreat. I knelt there in the woods and thanked Him for all that He had done for me in the past. I lifted Him up and exulted Him, praising His wonderful name and as I did, He lifted me up higher and higher, closer, and closer to His heart. I bonded with the One who left heaven so that I could experience moments like these. The best way I can define worship is to be totally one with Jesus, submersed in His love, filled with His grace, feeling the freedom that His forgiveness brings. He binds up my wounded soul and I truly live again in the freedom He brings to me. Then an attitude of gratefulness sweeps over my being and I want to give more and more to Jesus.

"I will lift up my eyes unto the hills from whence cometh my help. My help cometh from the LORD, which made heaven and earth."
Psalms 121:1, 2

Day Twenty-Eight

Typically, this portion of the book would describe another of my 30 days with Jesus, but this Sabbath was so filled with fellowship I will continue sharing my special Sabbath experience.

After wrestling with my love of the world and the things that were in it the apple, I ate was not sufficient to fill the void that was in my stomach. I felt a need for more nourishment. I went back to camp and lowered the food down from the tree. It was not much. I took some fresh grapes and started enjoying them.

"These grapes are extremely sweet, Jesus. Thank you for creating them. This bite is so juicy. You really do want us to find some enjoyment in life, don't You?"

"Yes, Don. I created men and women to find joy in living. Joy is one of the fruits of the Spirit. The more of My Spirit you have the greater will be your joy."

"What about sorrow, Lord?"

"In this world there will be sorrow but, in the world to come, it will pass away because its author will not be allowed to do his work of destruction." I popped some more grapes in my mouth letting them roll to the back where they were slowly devoured.

"Thank You, Jesus for the ability to taste and for all of the wonderful foods You have created for our enjoyment. It really is a blessing to have enough food to eat. I remember reading something David said that he had never seen the righteous forsaken or their seed begging bread. As far back as I can remember, there was always food enough to eat in our family.

I finished my fruit and toasted a couple of slices of bread over the newly rekindled fire. I sat there in meditation for a long time then turned to Jesus and asked Him to go with me on a hike. We would start walking around the lake. It was a small lake. Hiking around it would not take exceedingly long unless I paused to observe the handiwork of the Creator along the way. We started out.

How do You define a righteous person, Jesus?"

"From a human standpoint, Donielle, there is no righteous person. All have sinned and do not measure up to the glory of God. The righteous people David was talking about had been given righteousness. I gave it as a gift to them because they wanted it. It has to do with the direction a person is headed. If that person has decided to take their stand on the side of right, their goals change. They have a heavenly bent to their life. Since they are covered by My righteousness, The Father looks at them and sees My life transposed over theirs. I have chosen them, and they have chosen Me. A righteous person by this

*definition is blessed because they have chosen Me.
I place a hedge of protection around them. So long
as they remain in Me, the enemy has only limited
access to them. He can only work in their lives as
they give him permission through the making of
wrong choices.*

*Let Me give you an example. Suppose you
wanted to go on a trip. Before you took this trip,
you decided where you wanted to go. You may have
gotten a map out and charted your course. Before
you ever started your journey, your destination was
pre-determined. If you made all the right turns, you
would end up where you planned to go. A righteous
person has decided deep down inside of their heart
that they want to live a life that will result in eternal
life with Me. They are on the road to the Holy City.
Not all the righteous are at the same place on the
road to eternal life. Some are further along than
others, yet they all have one thing in common. They
are all going the same direction and so long as they
continue in the paths they have chosen will end up
in the same place. You have chosen this goal in your
life haven't you, Donielle?"*

"You know, Lord."

"Look up at the sky, Don. What do you see?"

"I see a deep blue that goes on to infinity."

"Is their more area beyond what you can see?"

"Yes, Jesus."

"How do you know?"

"Because of what I have read, Lord and have been told. I have been told this world is but a small globe in a universe so vast that it is but a spec in the cosmos."

"*That is true. How personal of a companion am I, Don?*"

"So far as I can tell, You are here with me personally and yet at the same time You are present in a million other places."

"*My Spirit has the ability to be in all places at all times. Do you remember the prayer that John recorded in the 17 chapter of his gospel?*"

"Yes, I recall reading that prayer several times."

"*The way the Holy Spirit can unify the righteous is by dwelling within all of them at the same time. Since the Holy Spirit is in one and the same Spirit in the others, they are one in the Spirit. It is a wonderful plan. When one person is led by the Holy Spirit, so is the other. One person then might have been given something that is needed by another member of the body. If the same Spirit dwells in each person then He can tell the one the needs of the other. That is how it was when My Spirit was poured out in the early rain. They had all things in common. Since all they had was considered a gift from God, they freely gave as what others had need. No one had need of anything because they shared all things between them. Today and even in the Christian church there is an undercurrent of thought that a*" *person or family needs to first look after their own needs before considering the needs of others. They accumulate large amounts of things they really do not need. When the Holy Spirit is poured out again in the latter days, the spirit of giving and sharing will again be a characteristic of the righteous. It will be possible because the Holy Spirit will again be uniting all as one.*

"How soon will that be, Jesus? From what I have heard You have appointed a time to judge the world."

"Many have asked that question and I will not give them an answer."

"Why?"

"Let us assume that the closing scenes of earth's history will start in three years. If My people knew they had three years before the culmination of the great controversy, what do you think they would do?"

"I suppose the reaction would vary with each Christian. Some would get busy and go to work for You. Some would procrastinate. Others may think they had much time they would try to see how much of the world they could live before it was gone."

"If people really knew when I was coming there would be some that did all you mentioned. There would be some who felt they had a special hold on this bit of information and would be selfish in their use of it. They would try to make certain their circle of associates was ready and would neglect sharing it

with the world. There will come a time when I will tell My chosen ones the day and hour of My return. At that time, conditions in the world will be such that My Spirit will make use of this knowledge to turn many to righteousness. The time is not right for that knowledge now though. The important thing is for you, Don to be always ready for when the beginning of the end comes, it will be in a time when very few are expecting it. Many will be caught unaware. It will be too late for millions because death will come to them and they will be swept into eternity, forever lost. Every hour, every moment you have with Me is precious. In the past, I have shared many things with you. You are aware of the signs and events that will surround the beginning of the end. You have also seen a brief vision of the scope of work My chosen ones will be given to perform and how long they will have to accomplish their mission. Be ready every moment, Don. You must keep watch; you must not let the enemy catch you in activities that are outside of Me. If I am not in you and you are not in Me, you are taking chances that could very well propel you into eternal loss. By eternal loss I mean lost from Me forever. If that were to happen to you and you realized too late that eternal life would not be yours, how important then would all your earthly treasures be, Beloved."

"They would have no value whatsoever, Lord. What would it really profit me if I were to gain the whole world at the loss of my soul? Do You really care so much, Jesus if one of the least of Yours is lost?"

"*Yes, Donielle. I care very much. If I could take everyone home with Me when I return. I would not want even the worst of sinners to lose out on eternal life. The glories that are to come, the forever life is so vastly superior to what you are experiencing now, there is no comparison. The enemy knows what those glories are like. He is doing all in his power to keep people enslaved in sin, to keep their minds from dwelling on the glories to come. He cloaks the truth around eternal life with mystery. He will take the common things and so clothe them with grander that people will sell their souls for nothing. On the last day, when they realize what they sold eternal life for, they will torture themselves for their stupidity. They will turn on those who deceived them with a wrath born straight from the heart of Satan. I wish I could shake My people awake. I would cry out to them day and night to make hast, to work out their salvation through Me with fear and trembling, fearful that they would lose out, and trembling with concern that their souls are one with Mine.*

When you were over there on the ground, pouring out your soul and crying to Me, I was right by you. Too many feel too secure in their place with Me. They feel they are Mine when they are far from Me. I wish I could share with you the work I have for you to do, Don. I could if you were willing, but you have not come yet to the place in your life where you are ready to give your all to Me. If I had My way with you, We would start tomorrow. We would have an adventure in faith that would stir the sleeping hearts of the saints. So many of My saints are sleeping. They have their houses and lands. They have their new cars and Recreation Vehicles. They have their retirement funds in earthly securities. But the day is coming when it will be gone in a moment. What then will those who have placed their trust in the things of this world?

"What about me, Jesus. How would I react if I lost my possessions?

"*You have your treasures, Don. You also have laid up a treasure in heaven. Were your possessions taken from you, you would turn to Me as naturally as the flower turns to the sun. Your wife would have a harder time. She needs to be surrounded by the security of a home and money in the bank. Soon these things will all be gone though. At that time many will lose their hold on Me.*

"You mentioned, Jesus there were many things You would like to talk to me about, but I am not ready to listen. Suppose I am to drop everything and launch out into that faith adventure you mentioned. What would be the first thing You would have me to do?"

"*There is much in your life that needs to be removed. Do you remember how many Bible characters were taken out of the stream of humanity for a few weeks, even a few years before they came into My service?*"

"I can think of a few, Jesus. Moses was twice 40 days and 40 nights up in the mountain. He also spent 40 years in the desert unlearning what he had learned in Egypt. You were led into the wilderness right after you came up out of the waters of baptism for 40 days and 40 nights. Elijah spent 40 days and 40 nights in the wilderness after running from Jezebel. Before that, he dropped out of mainstream humanity for 3 ½ years while You provided daily for his needs. Enoch spent weeks away from society seeking Your presence and found it. Paul also after being called, spent a few years seeking to learn all he could of You."

"That would be your first assignment, Don. I would provide a place away from the world for a time so we could develop a trust relationship with each other. I must come to the point where I can trust you, Son, even as you must come to the point where you will trust Me. This takes time but you have a foundation laid that is strong and sturdy. You are grounded in My Word. The rest of the building you have built on that foundation though has a lot of flaws. As a Master Carpenter, I have a lot of remodeling I need to do on that structure. We need time along together, but you are not ready for that now. A day will come when I will call you. Your Mother and Father's prayers are still registered in the books of heaven. I made a promise to your Mother, Don. I will do My best to see that your entire family are taken up to heaven when I return, but you need to set your priorities straight. If you diligently place Me first, best, and last in everything you do, this remodeling process will go very smoothly. If you do not it will take a long time. There are times when

I get one area fixed up and you come along and do some work on your own there without consulting Me. Then I must start all over again. Consult with me about these things, won't you?

"Yes, Jesus."

"*Not by might nor by power but by My Spirit. If you keep that in mind Donielle, you will complete the task I have planned.*"

Jesus and I finally arrived at a large rock looking out over the lake. There was a small hollow in it just the right shape to form a comfortable place to sit. I had packed my serviceman's Bible with me. The cover of the Bible was aluminum. It was a small box that contained the precious words of the companion by my side. I opened it up and was thumbing through it when a passage from Proverbs 3:33 (NSV) seemed to jump off the pages.

"*The curse of the Lord is in the house of the wicked, but He establishes the tent of the righteous.*

I did not know then that passage would be helpful early Sunday morning. A few day hikers came to the lake. There were a couple of other backpackers who were going higher to another alpine lake. I still had sore muscles and did not envy them in the least. After praying and talking with the Lord as well as listening for several hours, I went back to the tent and sat inside while I boiled some water. I decided to open a packet of soup and have it with more bread. The loaf that I brought would be about half gone after this meal. I also had a little desert. I brought along some cups of pudding. It would be a good meal. A little cheese on the bread dipped in fresh soup topped off with pudding was exactly what I felt my body needed.

After the meal I checked on the shirt. It was completely dry. I took it down and placed it back in my pack. It had been a wonderful day with my Savior. A good night's rest would be welcomed. So, after roasting a couple of marshmallows, over the last few embers. I retired to my tent.

About 3 in the morning, I was awakened by a sniffing sound rather close to my head. The animal was heavy. It made a lot of noise when it walked. When I stirred in my sleeping bag, it moved further away. What was it? On the way up I had a strange sensation in one area of the trail. It felt like eyes were watching me, Like I was intruding on some woodland creatures' territory. I thought of the paper about the bear but passed it by. this creature was a bear. He was circling my tent. He would sniff the air and move off a little then sniff again. I did not wish to have a one-on-one encounter with this woodland creature. What to do? I did have the assurance that Jesus was there in camp with me. That was helpful. But had he not also been in many camps where people were attacked by a bear? I had brought along a 22 pistol. Why? It was close. I reached into my pack and pulled it out. Then it dawned on me. I had placed my pack inside my tent before starting around the lake. I had also placed my food in it. It was not hanging from a tree out of reach from such creatures. It was beside me. At that moment I sent a silent prayer to the companion by my side.

"Jesus, I made a mistake. I did not take the proper precautions. Help!" It was then the passage from the rock came quickly to my mind.

"The curse of the Lord is in the house of the wicked, but He establishes the tent of the righteous."

"Thank you, Jesus, for this promise. You said it, and I believe it. If I am in you and You are in me then the discussion we had earlier is in effect, I am covered by your righteousness. If You have established my tent, Lord, no bear will be able to destroy it." And it was so. As my cry for help faded into the night air, I heard the heavy steps of that creature leave. The sound grew fainter and fainter as the distance between us became greater and greater.

"Thank you, Donielle for trusting Me. I am truly here with you. You are safe. Since you rest under My shelter, you will remain under the shadow of my strength. I am the one who will rescue you from evil. You need not fear any terrors by night nor arrows that fly by day. No deadly plague will fall upon you. A thousand may fall at your right side and ten thousand at your left but it will not come near your dwelling place. I have called you by name, Donielle. You are mine. So long as your trust is in Me, My promises will be sure. Thank you again for trusting me this morning. Remember. I am with you always, even unto the end of the world."

I crawled deeper into my sleeping bag and fell into a restful sleep with His promises fresh in my mind.

In this time with you, reader I have written the thoughts that came to me and the communion I shared while seeking God. I have also shared the experience with the bear. I do not know why this turned out the way it did. Surely the Angel of the Lord was close by protecting me from what might not have been a pleasant encounter. Did you know that the Angle of the Lord in the Bible often refers to Jesus Christ? In this instance a certain Bible passage had great meaning for me. Here it is. *The Angel of the Lord encampeth around about them who fear Him and delivers them.* Psalm 34:7. (KJV) You will notice I put a capital letter on Angel here in this passage. It was so. The Angel of the Lord was with me indeed.

So, what questions do I have now? What is it that my Lord wants me to do? I believe I know a way down deep within. I will not share these things with you. It is between me and my Lord. There is a place for you in His presence. I pray you will find His complete will for your life. He may ask you to take a great leap of faith and strike out on a work for Him that will require daily orders from the throne of grace. He may ask you to stay where you are and in your own corner let your light shine before those around you that they will see the good works He performs through you and give glory to God who is in heaven.

For God so loved the world that He gave His only Son, that whosoever believeth in Him, should not perish but have everlasting life.
John 3:16

Day Twenty-Nine

Greetings Friend, this is next to the last day I will be with you. Heaven is our goal isn't it? This is our hope. It is what we long for. Have you ever been to a family reunion? Was it exciting? I have been to several. It is better when you are close to the people you are reuniting with though. When there are a lot of people you do not see often, sometimes it can be awkward. This will not be the case in heaven though. There will be several reunions. Many of us have lost a mother or a father. There are some who have lost a brother or a sister. There are some who long for the day when that little one – who was ripped from their arms – will be returned. A few years ago, I wrote a book about heaven. I talked about it in the introduction chapter. I would like to share one chapter with you that talks about reunions. I long for the day when I will be reunited with my mother and father. They went to their rest trusting they would hear Jesus' call when He comes in the clouds of glory to claim His own. It will be a grand day when He calls them. Jesus will be so pleased at all the happiness there. Then the time will come when He takes each one of us to that beautiful home He prepared. He will point out all of the details and then He will say, "Welcome home, Don,

Welcome home, Catherine, Welcome home, William. Welcome home, Helen." What a great reunion to ever be with Jesus and the ones we love so dearly here on earth. May God bless as you let your imagination roam that better land that is to come, that land where we will see Jesus face to face and be re-united with our loved ones.

CHAPTER 7
HOMEWARD BOUND

There were several ways to travel in the Holy City. You could walk, fly, or glide along the surface a little above ground level. You could run without getting tired, or just hop and skip along. Nancy and Joy decided to skip along hand in hand. It was a beautiful sight to see them happy in their new-found love. There was plenty of time, so every now and then they would stop and talk to some of the people they passed. This is how they happened to come across the reunion of Adam's family.

Before we get into that portion of our story, however, I want you to grasp a little of the massive size of this city. If you started walking today and kept your average walking pace twenty-four hours a day, it would take you ten days to walk from one side of the city to the other. If you walked around the perimeter without stopping, it would take over a month. Therefore, our ability to travel there will be different than it is here on earth.

Much of Heaven was open. Families from all generations met in groups large and small for a reunion that need never end. Sometimes ten or twelve generations met in one group. One such group was the household of Adam and Eve. Abel was there, with Seth and all his children. Several other sons and daughters of Adam and Eve were there with their children, and their children's children, and their children's children, and so on. Eve was still carrying her little bundle of love when Nancy and Joy passed by this company of giants and went up to speak to them. Nancy was surprised at the size of this baby. Though it seemed small in the arms of its mother it was huge compared to the little baby she had held when Sherry was born. The baby, in fact, was larger than Joy. Nancy did not even reach the waist of Eve. Joy was even shorter.

Eve gently lowered the little one down for them to see. The baby smiled and took up a bit of Joy's hair in her little fingers. Then she laughed the neatest laugh. Joy beamed her one beautiful smile and gave a quick kiss right on a rosy cheek. Eve's baby daughter had large, beautiful eyes. Joy had never seen eyes so clear. They were as blue as the sky above the city and sparkled with the reflections of its beauty. Nancy and Joy left Eve and began to look around.

The beauties of the garden of Eden were everywhere. The home Adam had built was a model of loveliness. It rose out of the garden like a lovely plant. Vines were interspersed with differing kinds of fruit trees. The living foliage formed the structure of the home itself. You could pluck grapes from the kitchen wall or sample oranges while you rested on living furniture that bloomed with flowers and produced fruit of its own. Nothing had died before Adam and Eve were expelled from the garden so all the materials our first parents had used to create this home was either alive or in the form of a mineral or gem. There was another thing about the garden of Eden that was noticeable to Joy. There was a melodious sound that seemed to pulse through all of nature. Before sin, this musical sound pulsated in the whole earth. The trees and flowers loved it. Some would say it was music from the throne of God. When Adam and Eve sinned, a different song permeated the world. It was a song of sin and death. It had destructive power where the song before sin had living power. Joy could hear the living song now. She could feel it pulsing through her and with it, life eternal.

Joy tasted some of the dark, sweet cherries that grew by the doorway of Adam's home. She peaked in and saw the gold and silver furnishings generously laden with thousands of diamonds. Each diamond reflected the glorious light of heaven and transformed it into a myriad of millions of colorful rainbows. On tables of polished marble, she saw some of the oranges and tangerines Adam had plucked from his grove or perhaps the wall itself. She patted Adam's dog on the head, and he wagged his tail with delight.

Enoch came over to where they were and gave them a warm welcome. He was the oldest, continuously living human in the City, over five thousand years young. This was because the Bible tells us He was translated without seeing death from the earth before the flood. His son Methuselah was there and joined him. Methuselah was the oldest man that ever lived, nine hundred sixty-nine years to be exact. God in His great love chose to honor these two saints with long life. It was really something to see them side by side. They presented quite a contrast. Enoch bore a dark, youthful beard and Methuselah had a long, snowy white one that came well below his waist. A twinkle came to the eyes of the ancient saint as he saw Joy.

"So, you are the privileged one all Heaven is talking about, Charaeshera." He smiled a warm smile as he spoke her name.

"Who is talking about me?" asked the surprised little girl.

"I heard several mentions of your name as you came toward the garden. They saw you with Jesus."

"Yes, I was with Jesus. He showed me many wonders in Heaven today," responded the child.

"He came and took me up to His throne. It is so beautiful from up there. I could see everything in the whole city. I even saw Eve and her baby girl. The Father is nice too. He talked to me and told me why I could come to heaven."

"And why did He allow you to come to heaven?" questioned the ancient one.

"He said I was brought to heaven because I helped a lot of people, but I don't remember helping anybody. I only remember hearing of the story of Jesus and realizing how grateful I was for His love. I came to love Jesus because I could feel Him right by me every time I began to hurt or get lonely. I told Him I loved Him often. When other people complained of pain, or hurt like me, I told them Jesus loved them too. Some would ask me how I knew, and I told them I could feel Him near me, loving me. When He took me in His big arms, it was like going home. I felt those arms around me many times down on that old dark earth. I do love Jesus more than anyone else. But I love everyone else too. I am so happy to be here and be able to see all these beautiful things. Thank you, Jesus, wherever you are now." "I can see now why Jesus took you to see the Father," responded Enoch. "I came to love Jesus the same as you while on earth. We would go on long walks together. I too felt those big arms around me. Then one day He took me here and I have been with Him ever since, except when He came down to earth to live, and die. I missed Him greatly then. But now we are all here together. It is so wonderful. Jesus really is loving and kind to allow us the pleasure to be in His house forever."

Joy smiled and nodded in agreement, then looked toward one of the flowered meadows. There she saw a large table formed from living vines. An unusual event was taking place. Samson had wandered into the camp of Adam and had challenged him to an arm-wrestling contest. Most of the company looked on with smiling faces. The contest was not a matched one. Adam's arm was quite a bit longer than Samson's, so the strong man had his arm cradled in a coconut and the match was on. Adam was gaining fast. His muscles flexed strongly, and Samson's arm went down slowly until it was just about to touch the table. Then a very unusual thing happened. Slowly but surely Samson pushed the giants arm back into an upright position then back in the other direction until it nearly touched the table. At that point Adam returned their arms to the upright position. The contest was over.

"Well, Adam, you put out some good strength," commented Samson as he took a cluster of grapes from the vine table and ate them hungrily. "A few more months of this delicious food, however, and I will have you for sure." Adam smiled and commended him on his strength. Then with a twinkle in his eye he replied.

"You are a good contender my, friend. It looks like I am going to have to work out if I expect to maintain any kind of a lead around here for long." With that, the two clasped each other's hand in a gripping handshake and parted company.

Three little boys were looking longingly up at Muscle Man, admiring his physique. He knelt and told them to hop on his shoulders. Two of them scrambled on his huge frame, but the third was a bit too short. Samson picked him up, carried him on one arm, then ambled off with his admirers to the "Valley of the Giant Plants," just beyond the winding river. The children called it that and were especially fond of the place. There were huge plants that twisted and arched like some ultra- modern water slides. The youngsters spent hours going from plant to plant and frolicking amidst the assortment created especially for them. Samson was a favorite of these children because he always had an interesting story to tell and took time to listen when the little ones sought him out.

Nancy and Joy left the garden and took to the air now. Soon they were in view of the dazzling mansions. They came down next to one of the giant fountains and strolled around watching the otters play tag with the seals. Joy went over to the water and took a long drink from one of the streams that came spouting out of a golden pool. There was no sound of a pump. The water seemed to defy gravity itself. The clear liquid entered her mouth and slid down her throat, vitalizing her entire being with new vigor. There was something about this water that satisfied. It healed the very soul.

The two were at the entrance of the beautiful homes now. They paused a moment to look up at the glory of the sight before them. A golden street wound up to an archway made of transparent jasper. The colors of the archway were deep reds and oranges with dashes of yellow. At the top of the arch were inscribed words "HOLINESS TO THE LORD." Above the archway, stretching miles into the sky, were the beautiful homes of the Saints on this side of the city. The view took Joy's breath away. Her eyes, so darkened on earth, seemed starved for each beautiful scene. She had to touch, feel, and smell everything to see if it was real. She stood staring at the beauty before her for a long, long time, then spoke.

"These are the most beautiful homes in all of heaven!" she exclaimed in a whispered, reverent tone.

"They are beautiful," responded her new mother. "And higher than any mountain on earth. They are more glorious than ten of our suns. I never imagined such beauty could exist anywhere! It is amazing how Jesus has planted beautiful gardens all over these homes and filled them with millions of colorful flowers."

Among the gardens, brilliant birds swung from trailing vines loaded with grapes and fruit of rarest beauty. Their unceasing songs ascended to God with joy unquenchable. Other plants of varying shades of green and gold were interspersed among the flowers. At that moment there was a flash of red and green. The parrot glided to rest on Joy's shoulder. "Are you happy Joy? Are you happy you are going home?"

"Yes, Mr. Parrot, I am so happy I can't hold it in any longer." With that the little girl cried out from the depths of her very soul. "Thank You, Jesus, Thank You, and I Love You, and thank you, Nancy, for telling me about this place and the love Jesus had for a little cripple like me." She turned toward the throne as she spoke and caught a faint twinkle in the eyes of the Father as He looked down at her from His place high above. "This parrot calls me 'Joy'."

"What a nice name," smiled Nancy. "You are a joy to be with. May I call you Joy?"

"You may if you like," responded the girl. "Joy is exactly what my new name means, so I don't think Jesus will mind if you call me that. I am happy too and have lots and lots of joy inside me. It just must come out or I think I would explode. Heaven is so pretty, and everyone is so good to me. How could I be anything else but joyful?"

As if in a dreamland, Joy and Nancy started up the golden street into the mansions above. Higher and higher they went. The view changed from every angle. Wide verandas curved into spiraling stairs and winding hallways. Gold and silver archways framed the entrances to intersecting terraces and spacious courtyards. Glistening stairways opened into living gardens with flowing waterfalls and vibrant, green lawns. When they spoke out loud their voice returned to them, bouncing off the polished pillars and crystal walls. A hundred kinds of fruit spread their beauty before any who wished to eat them. Plums, peaches, apricots, and apples of gold and silver, beaconed to the hungry traveler; "Partake and be filled." The buzzing of bees blended with the beating wings of the ruby throated hummingbird. A little sparrow sang from his perch on the flowering branches of the wisteria vine. Gems of rarity and beauty sparkled from every nook and cranny. Joy found herself raising her voice with the singing birds as they went ever higher.

> "Thank you, Lord, for saving my soul.
> Thank you, Lord, for making me whole.
> Thank you, Lord, for giving to me,
> Your great Salvation so full and free."

Nancy joined her now and the two went singing upward, ever higher.

> "Thank you, Lord, for saving my soul.
> Thank you, Lord, for making me whole.
> Thank you, Lord, for giving to me,
> Your great Salvation so full and free."

They were accompanied by their echoes and distant thoughts. Each remembered singing that song on some of the long dark nights when a certain little girl could not sleep because of the pain in her scrawny legs. But the dark night of sin could not be remembered for long. They came to a wide veranda with a gold and silver table.

"Let's sit down for a moment, Nancy, I want to ask you about my family."

"Okay," responded the nurse. "What do you want to know?"

"Did you ever meet any of my grandparents?"

"Yes, on a couple of occasions I saw your mother's parents. Your Mother did not have much to do with them, but they came to see you at times when you were really little."

"What were they like? Were they nice?"

"Yes, they were very loving. It pained them to be treated so by their daughter. They loved her a great deal and wanted to be a part of her life. They would have gladly helped her bear the burden of your care, but Joyce would not let them even speak to you. Your Grandparents never got to hold you."

"Are they in Heaven, Nancy?" questioned Joy.

"Yes, they are, Joy. I saw them at the Supper. When the meal was over, they tried to find you. Where did you go?"

"First, I was with Trust, responded the girl. "He is my adopted brother. He sorts of looked after me on the great white cloud going to Heaven. He is an exceptionally good friend, and I love him very much. He is not with me now because they had a reunion of all the people that made up the stars in his crown. He has hundreds of stars. After leaving him with his friend Lasonaph, I was with Jesus. He took me to sit with Him on His throne."

"Jesus took you to His throne Joy?" questioned the surprised Nancy.

"Yes, He took me to meet the Father. It was all very grand and nice. I felt so small, though, next to those two great Kings."

"So, that is what you, Methuselah and Enoch were talking about? You must be special to Jesus if He took you to His throne so soon after the Supper," responded Nancy. "He must love you a great deal."

"He told me He loved me. Even the Father told me I had been an inspiration to many. I do not know what He meant by that, though. Who did I ever inspire, and how could a little blind, cripple girl like me, inspire anyone?" "Oh, but you inspired me a great deal, Joy. You inspired the doctors and nurses who took all those tests to determine if you could be helped. They all admired your happy, loving nature. You inspired all the sick people that ever roomed with you too."

"Well, I am glad then, that I acted happy. I did not feel happy sometimes, but when I acted happy, it made me happier. I hope I get to meet my grandparents soon. I would like very much to have a Grandmother and Grandfather." The two got up from the table and continued upward. At last, they were at the door of Joy's room. She gently touched it, and it retreated quietly into the wall. She looked inside with amazement. There, sitting on some of the exquisite furnishings, were her grandparents.

"We thought you would come here sometime," spoke up Grandfather. "You sure seem to be a busy little girl for all your short stay in Heaven. You are one little person who is hard to catch up with." Joy stared at the two saintly beings with a raptured expression on her face then burst forth with an excited voice.

"Grandmother! Grandfather! You are here! You are here in Heaven! Oh, I am so happy I will squeeze you tighter than you can imagine! Just let me get a hold of you and you will see what I mean!" She flew into their outstretched arms and hugged and squeezed and kissed them until she nearly turned blue. Grandmother finally spoke with tears of joy streaming down her rosy cheeks.

"You are just like my little girl coming home to me again, more beautiful than ever. You have your mothers' eyes, and that smile came from your Father, I know." He smiled like that at times, and I thought it was so beautiful. I must admit, he charmed me like no other man except your grandfather. It is so special to have you here, Sherry. You do not know how much we have missed seeing you. Now you are ours forever. Let me have some more of those hugs and kisses. I can't seem to get enough of you." With that Grandmother picked Sherry up and rested her on her sturdy lap. Joy looked deep into her loving face for a long time. She hugged and kissed her repeatedly then hopped into the arms of her waiting Grandfather. They surrounded her completely, and he kissed her while stroking her lovely curls with his big hands. Had she been tired she could have taken a nap, secure in his arms, but she was not tired. She did not know what the word tired meant since entering Heaven. The once forsaken, blind, crippled girl was at that moment the happiest little girl in all the Universe. She had a Mother, a brother, and two lovely grandparents that cared for her more than words can tell.

After all the hugs and kisses were given, Joy jumped down from her Grandfather's lap and looked around her home. It was beautiful. She reached into her robe, pulled out the fruit from the Tree of Life, and set it on a golden shelf. She also placed her crown there, and the stone Jesus had given her with her new name. Her palace was simply beautiful. There were many exquisite furnishings. She had two windows. She went to one now and looked out. There, not six feet away, was a quiet fountain. Joy loved fountains. Further out, toward the center of the city, she could see the tree of life towering into the air. Behind it was the great white throne. She looked up and saw Jesus had gone. He must be with others somewhere in the city. She got up on the windowsill, and a quick leap took her safely to the refreshing water. She let it spray her on the face, and over her hair causing her curls to form tight little ringlets. She drank some of this water. It tasted even better than the water from the great fountain. She took the flower out of her hair and replaced it with a brilliant pink one that grew next to the stream. Jesus had created a long water slide. Joy climbed to the top and slid down the slide, thoroughly soaking herself all over. She tried it again, and again and thrilled at the speeds she could attain by the time she reached the base. Joy looked back at the window and was surprised to see her grandparents and Nancy smiling down at her. She picked a grape, slowly ate it, then flew back in through the window. She took a more thorough tour of her palace. There was a living sofa that produced violet flowers. It was in the living room. The flowers had a sweet fragrance that perfumed the whole dwelling. They smelled like Lilly of the Valley. In the dining area was a table set with all manner of fresh fruit. Some she had never seen before. Her grandmother told her some of the fruit came from other planets.

"You mean there are different kinds of fruit on all the other planets?" asked Joy.

"Yes." Replied her Grandfather. "I brought some of these home from just such a planet yesterday."

"We will have to go to another planet and see these wonders." said Joy. The walls of the dining area were covered with various gems. Jesus had collected ones that were brightly colored. He knew Joy's eyes would love to drink in the resplendent colors. Being blind on earth had given her a special appreciation for beauty, and Jesus had spared no expense in furnishing her home with resplendent colors. There was a veranda off the dining area. The family went there. It was framed with a golden trellis, covered with delicate vines and beautiful flowers of every color imaginable. A cool breeze blew constantly there, and the mists from the waterfall made it a very refreshing place indeed. In the pools beneath the waterfalls there were colorful fish of several varieties. They swam in circular patterns spreading an iridescent shimmer throughout the whole pool.

Joy looked at the walls. They were made of mirrored gold. She could see her reflection perfectly on all sides. She could also see the reflections of all the little treasures there. To Joy, this was the most beautiful place in heaven. She went into her guest room. There were lots of shelves there. Some had interesting things on them, others were empty. She took the red roses Nancy had picked from the beautiful building and placed them in a crystal vase on one of the shelves. She looked admiringly at them. Truly heaven was the best and most beautiful place anyone ever could imagine, and she was the happiest little girl anyone could picture. Celestania looked quietly in from the open door and smiled as only a guardian angel can smile when he knows that all is well. The joy that animated from his little one's face was reward enough for a thousand angels. The memory of this little girl, so happy now with her new-found family, would remain in his mind as one of his most precious moments for all eternity. Joy was Home at last.

BIBLE TEXTS

"No human being has ever seen, heard or even imagined what wonderful things God has prepared for those who love Him." 2 Corinthians 2:9

"With this news bring cheer to all discouraged ones. Encourage those who are afraid. Tell them this, "Be strong and do not fear, for your own God is coming to destroy your enemies. He is coming to save you." And when He comes, He will open the eyes of the blind, and unstop the ears of the deaf. The crippled man will leap like a deer, and those who cannot speak will shout and sing! Springs will burst forth in the wilderness, and streams will flow in the desert. The parched ground will become a pool, with springs of water in the thirsty land. Where desert jackals lived, there will be reeds and rushes! And a main road will go through that once-deserted land; it will be named the 'Holy Highway.' No evil-hearted man can walk upon it. God will walk there with you; even the most ignorant cannot possibly miss the way. No lion will lurk along its course, nor will there be any dangers; only the redeemed of the Lord will go home along that road to Zion, singing the songs of everlasting joy. For them, all sorrow and all sighing will be gone forever; only joy and gladness will be there." Isaiah 35:3-10

"Do not lay up in store for yourselves treasure on earth, where moths and rust will come and destroy it, and where thieves can break in and steal all you have saved, but store up for yourselves treasures in heaven, where moth and rust do not destroy, and where thieves cannot break in and steal it, for where you have stored your treasure, that is where your heart will be also." Matthew 6:19-21

"How lovely is your dwelling, O Lord Most High! My soul yearns, even faints, for the courts of my God, my heart, and my soul cry out for the living God. Even the sparrow has found a home, and the swallow a nest for herself, where she may keep her young--a place near your altar, O Lord Almighty, my King, and my God. Blessed are those who dwell in your house; they will ever praise you." Psalms 84:2-4

"Blessed are those who place their strength in you, who have set their hearts on this pilgrimage. As they travel through the Valley of Baca, they will make it a place of springs; the autumn rains will also cover it with pools. They will go from strength to strength, till each appears before God in Zion." **Psalm 84:1-7**

Day Thirty

The last of our 30 days together has finally come. I suppose if there are 30 ways to end this book, there are 100 that I had an ending all made last evening. Just as I was about to go to sleep though, I pushed the wrong button and lost it all. Later I found out how I could have recovered the data with a couple of keystrokes, but it was too late by then. By morning I had another ending in mind. Perhaps this will be the right one. Yesterday we focused on the eternal world to come. My feeble attempt at describing it is less than a shadow of what God has prepared for us. It has been fun sharing with you. I would like you to know that I have prayed for you. I prayed for everyone who might pick up this little book. I claimed the prayer Jesus gave from the cross in your behalf. *"Father forgive them for they know not what they do."* That prayer of forgiveness from the lips of Jesus was for you and it was for me. It took in the whole world. I claimed the merits of the blood of Jesus as reason enough for Him to work in your behalf. I prayed that the Holy Spirit would come and visit you. I prayed that He would enter within and help you fight your spiritual battles. I prayed that Jesus would send His angels to you and cause any of the enemy's angels to retreat long enough that the Holy Spirit can speak to your heart. I prayed that since you are now justified through Jesus Christ, that He cover you with His robes of righteousness. I prayed that Jesus would cover you with the whole armor of God that every fiery dart the enemy sends you would be stopped before you are led into temptation. I prayed that as you read this book you will come to know Jesus in a very personal way. And finally, I claimed the promise in your behalf that states: *Being confident of this very thing, that he which hath begun a good work in you will perform it until the day of Jesus Christ:"* Philippians 1:6. Only God can cause His good work to be done in you. It is by His power alone. As victories are gained, He will be exulted and glorified.

In this last day with you I want to give you an invitation and make an appeal. We will again look ahead to the culmination of our hope in Jesus Christ. Shortly after my mother and father died, I was feeling homesick for them. It takes a while for the grieving to pass. While talking to Jesus about it I felt inspired to write out some of the feelings I might have when I am united with them again. Unlike the story of Joy and Trust this one is personal. It could be my story, or it could be yours. We are the characters in this drama. As you read this first-person account of what I felt when I considered the reunion with my parents, perhaps you can enter a portion of it. If you have lost your parents in death, you can be the one who meets them in this story. The aunts, uncles and cousins can be yours. Just cross out the names I supplied and place your own in the story. I will end as usual with a Bible text. May you personally hear Jesus speak the words of this text to you on that day when He comes in the clouds of heaven. This is my prayer. I will say goodbye now and may God bless you in your moment by moment walk with Jesus. The story is entitled "Don't lose out."

We had been on our way to heaven for several days. We were almost home. Just in front of us loomed that glorious city of God. It grew larger and closer with each passing moment. As I saw it, amazement overcame me. I had tried to imagine what it looked like but nothing on earth can be compared to it. Its towered miles into the sky. It was so tall; any earthly mountain would be dwarfed in comparison. A group of majestic angels made their way quickly to the front of the procession. I looked at the walls of Jasper and marveled at the glory that came flooding though their transparent surfaces. I saw the pearly gates and wondered at their splendor. Nothing evil or sinful could enter through them or survive the glory that shown from this place. This masterpiece of Jesus would be our home for eternity, and we cried.

"Hallelujah! Praise be to the Creator and Redeemer of heaven and earth."

As our eyes became accustomed to the brightness around us, they reached the very top of the wall and there we saw a company of angels. One group of angels had advanced ahead cried out in a mighty voice.

"*Lift up your heads O ye gates and be ye lifted up ye everlasting doors so the King of Glory may come in.*"

From the top of the wall the retina of angels answered.

"*Who is this King of Glory?*" The angels on the cloud answered.

"*The Lord strong and mighty. The Lord mighty in battle. He is the King of Glory.*" The angels on the walls asked the question, again the response came from those on the cloud. This time it was much louder.

"*The Lord mighty in battle. He is the King of Glory.*" As we neared those pearly gates they began to open slowly. Bright streams of brilliant light poured forth and illuminated the cloud we were on with a brilliance ten times brighter than any sun. As this happened, the attending angels began to separate the throngs of redeemed into 12 groups. I was directed to the gate of Zebulun. That was the one I was to enter. As I neared it, I thought back on the events that had taken place in the last week since our rescue from earth by Jesus. I remember watching as that small black cloud came ever closer and closer to the earth. It grew more and more glorious with each passing second. I remember seeing the wicked running with terror as they looked up and saw Jesus seated on the cloud. A look of indescribable horror twisted their faces. They cried for mountains, rocks, anything to come and hide them from the avenging face of Jesus. He answered their prayer, not by sending rocks or mountains but something else. As a mighty earthquake rocked the planet, huge chunks of ice fell from the angry clouds. Everything was taken out with the earthquake. No building was left standing. None of the righteous were struck though. The hail fell on all sides of them. At the same time huge cracks opened in the earth. Many of the remaining nonbelievers who had not been destroyed by the brightness of Jesus glory went down into the cracks and were swallowed up by the earth. I could not focus on the devastation for long. I wanted to see Jesus. He, above all beings, was the one who loved me most. He was the one who was my dearest companion and friend. He was the one who walked with me during the worst time of trouble this world had ever experienced. Yes, I wanted to see Jesus. Not only see Him but touch Him, embrace Him. Retreat to His waiting arms. Then I saw Him. It was then I realized how unworthy I was for Him to even consider meeting with me. I noticed His eyes. They blazed like fire and before their all-consuming gaze, my life was laid bare before me. There was nothing, absolutely nothing I had done that could ever make me worthy of such a King. I could not remember any sins though I knew I had been a great sinner and cried.

"The Lord has come and who will be able to stand?" Then I heard a voice, rich and melodious answer.

"*Those who have clean hands and a clean heart. They will be able to stand.*" I looked at my body then, and in a moment, it was changed. Life everlasting surged through my being like so many tiny streaks of lightning. Every cell came alive with a vitality never experienced. I found myself shouting out loud.

"Hallelujah! Glory be to God." I remember taking my glasses from off my face and flinging them to the earth. How I had managed to keep them through all the turmoil of those last few months was beyond me, but one thing was certain, I had no need of them now. I again turned and looked at Jesus. His eyes softened for a moment and He spoke directly to me.

"*My grace is sufficient for you Don, enter into the joy of your Lord. Your sins have been blotted out by My blood. Enter into My rest.*"

At that moment nothing else mattered. I had made it. Heaven was certain and I knew I could spend eternity with Jesus and love every precious moment I had in the presence of this Kindly King. When the realization of that struck me fully, I cast myself on the ground and worshiped the Creator who was seated beside the Father on the throne.

After some time, I looked at the Father. He was in the exact likeness of Jesus. They appeared to be twins except the father looked older somehow. Jesus was more youthful and His bearing kinglier. A dazzling crown of glory rested on His head. No crown of thorns now scarred that lovely face. Then a million shouts of glory ascended from the waiting saints as the Jesus drew even nearer to the earth. The cloud came to stop and a silence like death itself spread over the earth. The large black clouds that had moments before spied forth their deadly missals of frozen death, stopped their angry bellowing. The lightning and thunder ceased. The earth stopped quaking. All nature became silent before the awful presence of its Creator. Jesus then cried with a mighty voice that rocked the very foundations of the earth. It rolled from one end of heaven to the other then echoes came back from around the world.

"Awake, awake, you who sleep in the dust. Awake and live forevermore."

That voice penetrated the ears of the dead. I looked over the broken surface of the earth and it appeared to boil like a pot as millions and millions of people came from their dusty graves and were caught up into the air to meet Jesus. There were people of giant stature in that vast throng, antediluvians who had talked face to face with Adam. There were men who had given their lives for their countries. There were those special people who had been called to give up their life for the sake of the truth. These martyrs came out from the earth praising the Lord of Glory. There were little children and babies in that throng. I saw a dear mother being lifted into the air and a bright, shining angel bore two little ones to her waiting arms. She wept for joy as she saw her babies restored, perfectly whole to her outstretched arms. The little one's dad joined her now. He had come up from his own dusty grave, the curse of sin forever gone. They wrapped their arms tightly around each other and praised God.

I remember looking for my Mother and Father in that throng. I had waited and longed for this moment when they would be restored to me, but I was separated from their resting place by over 2000 miles. I was driven by an overwhelming urge to search for them but how could I find them among so many? I was surrounded by millions and millions of people. How could anyone find anyone? Just then my feet were lifted from the ground and I looked up into the face of my guardian angel for the first time. Love shown from his radiant image and he said I will take you to your parents. As we rose higher and still higher into the heavens, off to the left I saw my wife, Patty was also being carried by a mighty angel. She was united with her family. Then my angel and I made our way to where my sweet little Mother waited for our approach. It was wonderful to see her again. Dad was by her side and when they saw me a smile as broad as their faces graced their shining countenance. I jumped from the arms of my angel and embraced those dear people who had given me life. A hundred tears of joy were shed as we praised God together for His goodness. I thrilled with the thought that there would be no more goodbyes. We need never be separated again.

Mother was beautiful now. The deforming arthritis that had twisted her body was gone. She was more youthful than a 16-year-old girl. The wrinkles I had probably placed on Dad's brow were all erased, and as the cloud ascended higher and still higher, my sister, Helen joined us, and we all locked our arms together in a loving embrace. What joy we had as we rose further and further into the heavens, praising God for His goodness and wonderful love. We were especially thankful because all our families were on the cloud. Not one was missing. My son was brought to us by his own angel and the sons and daughter of my sister followed shortly thereafter. It was then I realized more than ever before the power of prayer, for it was the prayers of those dedicated parents that had brought us safely through to the kingdom of God. After a while Aunt Helen came up with Uncle Charlie. I remember the last time I saw her. Now she was changed. She was gorgeous. She still had a beautiful crown of white hair. Helen Marie and I both went up and embraced her in a loving hug. It was so good to see these folks again, all of them. On earth we had known love but somehow on this cloud, going heavenward, love was magnified a hundredfold. The depth of feeling we had known no bounds. Joy unspeakable, eternal like nothing ever before experienced raced through us. If eternity were like this, it would be more wonderful than any conceivable thought or imagination. What love, what wonderful love.

Earth was retreating quickly now. It was but a speck. We could not get away from it fast enough. Over the next several hours this mighty procession made its way heavenward as shouts of praise and gladness ascended from millions and millions of voices. Then I was walking through that gate. The angels had arranged us in a giant rectangle. I was well back from the front. Jacob's son, Zebulun lead my procession with his immediate family close behind. As I passed through the gate, the beauty of that glorious city struck me full in the face. Mansions of indescribable splendor towered into the heavens. Crystal spirals graced every corner. In the center of the city, rising high above everything else, was the awesome throne of God. As we neared the city, it had been lifted above the walls and came to rest in its location in heaven. At that time Jesus had dismounted the throne and stood below it as the redeemed of all the ages advanced toward Him. As He saw them coming, a look of love and satisfaction graced His face. We all could read His love for us. It was wonderful. After looking at Jesus again I glanced around at the city. High above the Father a brilliant rainbow surrounded the throne. My eyes traveled outward, and I saw the River of Life flowing from the base of the throne. It split into 4 parts and headed in 4 different directions. Golden canals formed the boundaries of the rivers. Each canal flowed down the center of a street of transparent gold. At the beginning of one of the canals stood the Tree of Life. It towered high into the heavens and reached nearly to the height of God's throne. Its trunk appeared to be made from transparent gold mixed with silver. In other parts of the city, trees towered into the heavens. They were gigantic. Some reached nearly to the top of the walls. Birds of paradise filled the skies. Twelve flocks of snow, white doves flew in formation over the processions coming in from each gate. They spelled out the words.

"VICTORY!" Then they changed and the words, "GLORY BE TO THE FATHER, AND TO THE SON, AND TO THE HOLY SPIRIT." Then "VICTORY!" Was again spelled. Off to the sides of the broad streets of gold were fields of beautiful flowers. Giant animals grazed peacefully in the evergreen meadows and the atmosphere was charged with a living current that vitalized everything with a vitality akin to nothing I had ever experienced. We were home in a place more glorious than words can portray. The beauty and splendor were beyond imagination. This would be our habitation forever and ever. We would live with our Lord, and Savior, Jesus Christ, forever and ever. Eternity stretched before us, unending. The angels must have been thinking the same thoughts because they were unable to remain silent a moment longer. They broke forth in melodious strains of rapture. Everyone was inside the city now. We all joined in the song of praise. The melody was so loud the very foundations of the New Jerusalem rocked as we sang on and on.

Suddenly the vast throng became silent again. Jesus had raised His hands. He was about to speak. All eyes were fastened on Him. We could see Him clearly. His form seemed to rise above the vast assembly. We looked and saw the nail prints in His hands and feet and with one motion cast ourselves down on the golden streets as we realized the price He paid for our redemption. We dare not rise until His voice. Rich and loud, like many waters, cried out.

"Arise!"

We stood to our feet. Looking first at us then up to the Father seated on the throne, Jesus spoke.

"*I have finished the task You gave Me to do Father. These are those I have redeemed from the earth. I am asking that You accept them into this kingdom of glory forever and ever. I want them to be with Me wherever I go.*"

Rising His nail pierced hands up to the Father, He again spoke.

"*I shed My blood for them. They are Mine. I purchased each one with My blood.*" At that time, we again fall prostrate on the streets and worshiped Jesus as we realized He had given everything He had to assure us a place with Him in this beautiful home. Then from the throne a voice came loud and clear.

"*It is enough. The price has been paid. I will accept these, Our children into this kingdom. Well done Son. I will give You what You have asked for. They will be Yours forever and ever. You have purchased them with Your own blood. They may enter into our joy, into our rest."*

Once again Jesus bid us rise to our feet. The procession moved ever closer to the loving Savior and we were united to Christ in ties that would never be broken while the angels sang anthem after anthem of praise and thanksgiving. Never again would death or sin touch us. We were safe. We were safe in the arms of Jesus, safe from the enemy of our souls. Lucifer, that Prince of Darkness would never again have power over any of us. He could never cause us to suffer again and we all cried,

"Hallelujah! Salvation belongs to our Lord and Savior, Jesus Christ. He is worthy of honor, and power, and glory, and praise. We will worship Him." He alone came to seek and save us who were lost. He alone, but alone no longer, for we were with Him and He was with us.

After that we all headed for different parts of the city. On the way I met Gary. He told of a reunion we were having with all the Hills. He said if I saw any of them to spread the word. We were to meet north of the Tree of Life after the worship service. I caught a glimpse of Bill and told him then I saw Uncle Glen and told him, but he already knew. He challenged me to a foot race. I ran faster than the wind but could not keep up with him, not even with my longer legs.

He was flying over the lawns of that eternal city. At last, I called out to him that I could not keep up and he slowed down, and we walked arm in arm for a way until he met up with Aunt Katy and then we parted. A reunion in heaven. That would be so great wouldn't it? The Joy that we experience in that place beyond the blue will be a joy that we cannot now comprehend. One thing will be certain. As we look back on our little stay here on earth, with its sin and troubles, we will know that this heavenly paradise was worth every sacrifice we had to make to attain entrance to its glorious realms. Heaven is cheap enough. It is ours for the taking. Jesus has done everything He can to make it accessible to us. The rest is up to us. Will we reach out and accept this gift that He offers? He has opened the doors for us. By faith we can enter that city and eat of The Tree of Life. Are you homesick for Heaven, Reader?

THE SPIRIT AND THE BRIDE SAY, "COME." AND LET HIM WHO HEARS SAY, "COME." WHOEVER IS THIRSTY, LET HIM COME. AND WHOEVER WISHES, LET HIM TAKE THE FREE GIFT OF THE WATER OF LIFE. REVELATION 22:17

Drink deeply, friend, drink deeply. That River of Life is flowing for you now. Drink deeply, and thirst no more. Heaven is cheap enough. Its glories are for you. Jesus is calling you, Mothers and Fathers. Jesus is calling you, Children. Jesus is calling you, Reader. Are you suffering from some lingering illness? Jesus is calling you to a place where sickness cannot exist. Is there trouble in your home–perhaps between you and your spouse? Jesus is calling you to a heavenly family where trouble is not known. Are you facing financial troubles? He has streets of gold and a golden crown for you. Are other troubles surrounding you that seem to shut out the glories of Heaven? Jesus is there beside you and He will lead you out of any difficulty or give you His strength to endure it. You who have been used to seeing with four eyes. He has new eyes that will never grow dim. Your glasses will not be needed in Heaven. Those with false teeth, He has a new pair of teeth for you and will give them to you before you eat of the Tree of Life. Have you lost a loved one in death's grip? By the grace of God, you will see your loved one again in that eternal abode with the saved. Is there a wayward child who seems bent on breaking your heart? The Tender Shepherd is seeking that lost lamb and He will do all in His power to see that son or daughter walk with you in Paradise. To miss Heaven will be to miss everything. The trial that is now pressing you down will be nothing then. What matters most is that you will be with Jesus forever. Eternal Life! Think of it. You will live forever and ever, never to die! That youthful body you had will be with you forever! Those who are dear to you can be with you forever. The Heaven experience can be your experience! It will be your experience! It must be your experience! You have an inheritance waiting for you. Take hold of it now! Jesus Himself has invited you. Join me in prayer now as we approach The Throne of Grace.

Our Father in Heaven. We realize that to be a citizen of Your Kingdom we have but to reach out and accept the gift of Eternal Life that You offer. We want to do that just now. We realize we cannot enter that city if we have anything in us that defiles. Search us just now. Notice each sinful desire, each cherished idol, notice everything that is separating us from You. We give these separating sins to Jesus just now and ask His forgiveness. We cannot remove them from our lives. It is beyond our power, but Jesus can remove them and has already done so. We accept the forgiveness that Jesus made possible by shedding His blood on Calvary. We stand beneath that crimson flood and allow it to wash all our sins away. If sometime in the future temptations surround us and we appear about to fall into sin, flash a bright picture of the glorious city into our minds so we will lose sight of the sin and catch a glimpse of our salvation. As we compare the temptation to the glory, we will receive the strength we need to overcome. If we are still tempted after seeing the glory, show us your face Jesus. Show us your face. When we sin, Your brow is covered with that cruel crown of thorns. But when we gain the victory through the power of Your blood, we see you crowned with a crown of glory, exulted above all things. May this picture of You be the one that we see.

Jesus, we want to walk with You here on earth, moment by moment. We know you have made Yourself available to us. You are beside us, within us and around us. Open the communication lines, Jesus. May we talk with each other as friends. Give us Your love for the lost and perishing ones next to us. Send Your Holy Spirit to minister to them through us. Use us to further Your kingdom here on earth, and by making ourselves available for Your service, we realize that You will come for us that much sooner. We trust You to give us the strength we need to overcome and one day soon be ushered into Your presence on that great, white cloud that will remove us far from this earth of sin and woe and take us to our heavenly home, ever to be with You. Even so come, Jesus. Come soon. In Jesus name we ask this. Amen.

DON'T LOSE OUT, FRIENDS!
DON'T LOSE OUT!

Matthew 25:34

"Then shall the King say unto them on his right hand, Come, ye blessed of my Father, inherit the kingdom prepared for you from the foundation of the world."

CPSIA information can be obtained
at www.ICGtesting.com
Printed in the USA
BVHW070737070421
604343BV00003B/356